LATIN AMERICAN
MUSIC

INDIAN BLOWING CONCHSHELL
By Jesús Carranza, Guadalajara, Mexico

Latin American Music
Past and Present

By

ELEANOR HAGUE

The Fine Arts Press, Santa Ana, California, 1934

Republished by Blaine Ethridge—Books, 1982

13977 Penrod   Detroit, Michigan 48223   U.S.A.

Please write for a free annotated catalog of books on Latin America, ethnicity, bilingual education and bilingual books for children.

Except for several minor changes, this new edition is a photographic facsimile of a copy in the Music and Performing Arts Department of the Detroit Public Library.

COPYRIGHT, 1934
By
ELEANOR HAGUE

**Library of Congress
Cataloging in Publication Data**

Hague, Eleanor.
　Latin American music.

　Reprint. Originally published: Santa Ana, Calif. :
Fine Arts Press, 1934.
　Bibliography: p.
　1. Music — Latin America — History and criticism.
I. Title.
ML199.H14 1982　　　　　780'.98　　　　82-2540
ISBN 0-87917-083-2　　　　　　　　　　　AACR2

Prayer

TO THE GOD PACHACAMAC
from
ANCIENT CIVILIZATION OF THE ANDES
By
Philip A. Means

O Pachacamac:
Thou who hast existed from the beginning,
Thou who shalt exist until the end,
powerful but merciful
Who didst create man by saying,
"Let man be."
Who defendest us from evil,
And preservest our life and health,
Art Thou in the sky or upon the earth?
In the clouds or in the deeps?
Hear the voice of him who implores Thee, and grant his petitions.
Give us life everlasting, preserve us, and accept this sacrifice.

ILLUSTRATIONS

TABLE OF CONTENTS

foreword

The plan on which this study has been laid out shows the chronological development of music in the Latin-American * countries. This method has come about because of the difficulty of finding material for the early part of the study. And even for modern times this difficulty holds true for some of the countries. The material for the first chapters is to be found only in the most fragmentary form in the works of the historians and travellers. For the later times, some of the countries have begun to make systematic studies and others have not. Therefore much of the work has been real pioneering with the joys and defects of all pioneering. But after everything is said and done the main interest lies in the growth of Latin-American * music as a whole, and each of the countries has had a part in the sum total.

The illustrations have been gathered from a variety of sources, including modern photographs and old prints and engravings. The modern photographs show, as only the camera can catch them, festival ceremonies that are still being performed in the remote parts of the continent. The prints from old books of travel and history, are full of detail that is sometimes accurate, and again fanciful to a degree that makes them unconsciously humorous. But they have real value in showing the impressions which the wonders of the new world made on the early readers in Europe. These prints were probably made from sketches or descriptions given to the European engravers by the returning travellers. The influence exerted by Rubens on the art of Europe is obvious.

Five friends have contributed the photographs; Mr. and Mrs. Guy Edwards, who spent several years in the highlands of Peru; Mr. Arthur Francis Bennett whose work has taken him to the northwestern corner of Argentina near the Bolivian frontier; and Dr.

---

* NOTE: The terms Latin-American, Spanish-American, or Ibero-American are used in this book, not because they are the ideal words to express that civilization which has a Spanish or Portuguese background in contrast to an Anglo-Saxon, but because up to the present time no better word seems to have been invented. A hyphenated word can never be completely satisfactory, but it is essential to have a term both brief and inclusive.

Foreword

Robert Hegner of Johns Hopkins University who had the good fortune to be present at a couple of fiestas in Bolivia. Miss Frances Toor of Mexico City was kind enough to give the two pictures of the Yaqui deer dancer. Their generosity and helpfulness are herewith gratefully acknowledged, for they were kindness itself.

Many of the illustrations of old prints were made from photostats taken at the H. E. Huntington Library at San Marino, California. The courtesy shown by every one connected with that institution makes one's contact there a very great pleasure.

To the several friends who have painstakingly read the manuscript, Mr. Henry C. Niese, Mr. and Mrs. Edwards, Miss Calista Rogers, and others, I tender my best thanks, as well as to the Officers of the Pan American American Union in Washington. Without the loan of some of their books and their help and advice the book could never have been written.

Chapter One

THE PEOPLE AND THE COUNTRY

LATIN-AMERICAN music means many things to many people; one to the primitive Indian in the wilds of the jungle or the high valleys of the Andes, and quite another to the educated dweller in Rio de Janeiro or Buenos Aires or Santiago. To the average citizen of the United States it usually means a genial familiarity with two or three songs of the type of *La Paloma* or *Estrellita,* without any great attempt to make further discoveries. It is quite true that Latin-American music includes all of these types and many more besides. For the Indian has his primitive tunes which he sings or plays, still using the instruments of past generations, and acting on his ancestral superstitions. The *Mestizo* has his music, and the educated city-dweller has the musical background of both Europe and America to draw on, and often knows these sources thoroughly. But all this variety of material lends greater charm to the study of the music, for one may approach it from many angles, that of the musician or the historian, the anthropologist or folklorist. For such an approach it is essential to understand what music has meant and does mean in the lives of the people.

So we shall glance in passing at the geographic surroundings of the different races and their varying modes of life, and see whether the individuals live in a state of freedom or bondage, peace or revolution, formalism or independence of thought. Modern political boundaries are of importance to the present study only in so far as they influence these conditions, and that will explain the apparently ruthless neglect of such boundaries here. Moreover, the differences between a nomadic or a sedentary life, an agricultural or a seafaring existence, the loneliness of virgin solitudes, or the turmoil of cities are all of importance in our consideration of the subject; as well as such purely geographic factors as climate, mountains, jungles, plains, islands, and so on.

All these conditions are found in one part or another of Latin-America. The various subdivisions, Mexico, Central America, the Antilles, the Philippines, and South America each form natural units; and for our purposes the continent of South America may be further divided in the following manner:—The Andes region, with an occasional distinction to be made between the northern and southern sections; the region of the Pampas, those wide rolling prairies different from and yet in a general way comparable to our own plains; and the huge region drained by the Amazon and Orinoco. In the latter are vast stretches of hill and mountain country, but for our purposes the region may be called a unit. The coastal cities make a fourth group. These natural divisions are made by obvious physical barriers, and the airplane is only beginning the slow process of breaking them down.

In considering the period which preceded the arrival of the Spaniards, one could easily be inveigled into fields that really belong to the archaeologist rather than to the music-lover. So we must leave aside such fascinating questions as the probable Asiatic origins of the race,[1] or that of the successive migrations of population which for the sake of sustenance, had to follow the everchanging climatic conditions.

We will use as a starting point the Indian races as they were when the Spaniards found them. At that time there were races in every degree of culture, from those highly developed ones whose names are familiar to any high school student,[2] such as Inca, Maya, Toltec and Aztec, to the most primitive types. Even today, the descendants of some of the latter remain primitive, and go under the general heading in Spanish of *Indios Bravos* or wild Indians. They will be treated in a chapter by themselves, as the modern anthropologists and travellers give more satisfactory accounts of their music and their customs in general, than do the early writers whose works are the sources of the present chapter. A sympathetic and inquiring outlook is more apt to be part of the anthropologist's equipment

[1] See **The American Indian,**—Clark Wissler. 2nd Ed. 1922. New York, also, **The Conquest of Brazil,** Roy Nash, P. 6 et seq. and others. One interesting link is to be found in the fact that the shell trumpet belonging in the Polynesian Islands and in South America is known as **pututu** in both regions.

[*] The first Mayan date has been worked out as 613 B. C.

[2] Humboldt gives as a first date for the Toltecs, 648 A. D., Nahualtecs 1178, Aztecs 1196.

than of the conquerors or even the missionaries.

The characteristics of these races are widely divergent. The more civilized had reached the agricultural stage of development; and the Incas in Peru, Mayas in Yucatan, and the groups in Mexico all had complex systems of government. They were splendid builders, and skilled in sculpture, metal-work, weaving and other crafts. Although their music would seem primitive and unsatisfactory to us, yet they had reached a point where they were no longer content merely with instruments of percussion. They had all begun to develop instruments with melodic possibilities, and also types of ceremonial music which implied forms and conventions. They had music that expressed various personal emotions. In spite of all these apparent similarities of custom between the races, which might suggest that a racial relationship existed, the archaelogist Brinton and other scholars state that the language roots do not show such relationship, which, if existing at all must have been extremely remote.

The first descriptions of their lives and music are to be found in the reports of the early Spanish writers, who gave detailed accounts of what they saw about them, and these accounts are so vivid that without apology we quote them in their own words throughout the chapter. The earliest description that is of interest here, concerns the music of the early Peruvians and was written by the half-breed Garcilaso Inca de la Vega. (1539-1616).[3] He says—

"In Musick they arrived at a certain Harmony, in which the Indians of Colla" [the basin of Lake Titicaca in Bolivia and Peru.] "did more particularly excell, having been the inventors of a certain Pipe made of Canes glued together" [that is panpipes, similar to the ancient Greek and Oriental instruments,] "which having a different Note of higher or lower, in the manner of organs, made a pleasing Musick by the dissonancy of sounds, the Treble, Tenor, and Basso exactly corresponding and answering each to other. With these pipes they often plaid in consort, and made tolerable Musick, though they wanted the Quavers, Semiquavers, Aires and many Voices which perfect the Harmony amongst us. They had also other Pipes, which were flutes with four or five stops, like the pipes of Shepherds; with these they played not in consort but singly, and tuned them to

---

[3] The edition of **The Royal Commentaries of Peru** here used is the Ricaut translation of 1688. P. 84.

sonnets, which they composed in metre, the subject of which was Love, and the Passions which arise from the Favours or Displeasures of a Mistress. These musicians were Indians trained up in that art for divertissement of the Incas, and the Curacas who were his Nobles; which as rustical and barbarous as it was, it was not common, but acquired with great Industry and Study."

Another description of pre-Spanish conditions, although written at a somewhat later date and about Mexico, is the following by Clavigero,[4] who says, "Their music was still more imperfect than their poetry. They had no stringed instruments. All their music consisted in the *Huehuetl,* the *Teponaztli,* horns, seashells, and little flutes or pipes which made a shrill sound. The *Huehuetl* or Mexican drum, was a cylinder of wood more than three feet high, curiously carved and painted on the outside, covered above with the skin of a deer, well dressed and stretched, which they tightened or slackened occasionally, to make the sound more sharp or deep. They struck it only with their fingers, but it required infinite dexterity in the striker." (See illustration.) Of the *Teponaztli,* Clavigero says "that it was also cylindrical and hollow, but all of wood, having no skin about it, nor any opening but two slits lengthwise in the middle, parallel to and at a little distance from each other. It is sounded by beating the space between these two slits with two little sticks, similar to those that are used for modern drums, only that their points are covered with *ule* or elastic gum," (Probably rubber,—E. H.) "to soften the sound. The size of the instrument is various, some are so small as to be hung around the neck, some of a middling size and some upwards of five feet long. The sound which they yield is melancholy, and that of the largest so loud that it may be heard at the distance of two or three miles. To the accompaniment of those instruments. . . . . the Mexicans sang their hymns and sacred music. Their singing was harsh and offensive to European ears, but they took so much pleasure in it themselves that on festivals they continued singing the whole day."

Another early writer, Bishop Landa of Yucatan, (1524-1579) speaks of the instruments he found among the Mayas, as "small kettledrums, played with the hand, and another made of hollow wood, played with a wooden stick, with a small ball on the end made

---

[4] The History of Mexico, Vol. 2 P. 207, Edition of 1817.

CEREMONY WITH ACTORS IN COSTUME

Two kinds of drums and rattles, according to Fray Diego Durán, 16th century. Courtesy of the Los Angeles Public Library

FLUTES, TRUMPETS, PANPIPES, CONCH

WHISTLING JARS

Photographs by courtesy of the American Museum of Natural History,
New York City

from the milk of a certain tree. (Again, probably rubber,—E. H.) They have long slender trumpets fashioned from hollow sticks with gourds fastened at one end. Another instrument is made from a whole turtle shell, which is played with the palm of the hand and emits a melancholy sound. They have whistles and flutes of reed or bones of deer, and from large snail shells. These instruments are played for their war dances."

The preceding quotations refer specifically to Peru, Mexico and Yucatan, but it is significant that these descriptions are apropos of many parts of Latin America.

From such writings we can begin to realize some of the elements of the indigenous music; the instruments, methods, and emotions the people wished to express; for as will be noticed, the descriptions cover both ceremonial music and personal customs. We have already mentioned some of the instruments, which, among the principal races, include not only percussion instruments but those capable of producing melody as well, although the latter were of such a simple character as greatly to limit the music performed. For it is a recognized fact in music, that whereas singers in reality have entire freedom to employ whatever scales they might wish, yet habitually they limit themselves to the scales of the instruments they are accustomed to hearing. All the early authorities agree as to the existence of the same types of instruments in Mexico, Central America, and the southern continent; drums of various kinds, big and little; rattles, whistles, flutes and trumpets, and also something in the nature of a jews-harp. The Incas also had panpipes and whistling jars, made of pottery. (See illustration.) A wide variety of materials was used in the making; stone, wood, bone, animal horns, clay, reeds, seashells, gourds with pebbles or seeds inside for rattles, and so on. Sometimes the Spaniards in describing the instruments they found, casually used some familiar name which is misleading to us. Thus Garcilaso describes a battle between the army of the Inca Viracocha and the Chancas at the siege of Cuzco, and says that, "Both armies remained the whole night upon their guard with sentinels set on each side; and in the morning by break of day the squadrons armed themselves, and with great noise of shouts and sounds of trumpets and timbrels and cornets, they began the onset." Here the name cornet was used for what was probably a primitive instrument of reed which really belonged to the oboe family. Simple instruments of this character are still to be found among some of the uncivilized tribes.

None of these accounts gives any indication of the existence of stringed instruments prior to the Spanish invasion, and the consensus of opinion seems to be that the Spaniards introduced them.

Illustrations of old instruments may be found as decorations on ancient pieces of pottery and metal ornaments, as well as in the ancient codices, a few of which still exist in museums. Actual instruments also may be found in some museums, notably a collection, mainly of Incan construction, in the Museum of Natural History in New York City. Mr. Charles W. Mead, formerly its curator, tested the flutes and took down the scales of twenty-six.[5]

Among the notations which he recorded, three flutes gave out only four notes, five had six holes, one seven, two had eight and one nine. Thirteen show a five-tone scale; this may often be approximated by the black notes of the piano, and is the scale most used among primitive races. This would indicate that on the whole a five-tone scale seemed to those people a desirable one. But, in the case of the Indians, the five tones were often far from accurate in pitch, according to our standards. The intervals represented by these holes vary considerably, and it is interesting to find that in some of the instruments a hole has been cut and then plugged again, and another cut nearby; indicating an evident desire to find a certain combination of sounds but inadequate means for accomplishing the purpose. In the present day, with more accurate tools, the Indians make excellent instruments.

The best modern scholars, D. Alomia Robles, A. Villalba Muñoz, Margúerite Béclard-D'Harcourt, C. W. Mead and others agree that a five-tone scale was the usual indigenous one, and that any one of the five notes might at one time or another be used as the keynote or tonic. Certain writers suggest that the changed relations resulting between the intervals, made scales that were considered to correspond to different emotions.[6]

Garcilaso tells us that among the Quichua Indians, "Song had

[5] See his pamphlet, "The Musical Instruments of The Incas, as supplement to the Museum's bulletin, July, 1903.

[6] Compare the use among the East Indians of their **Ragas**, also the Greeks use of their modes. Among the North American Indians a given

it's recognized scale or character, so that a lover playing the flute to his lady-love, could indicate to her and to the world in general, his contentment or discontent, favor or disfavor, as if conversing with the flute." He also says that "the songs they composed of their wars and great achievements were never set to the aires of their flute, being too grave and serious to be intermixed with the pleasures and softnesses of love; for those were only sung at their principal festivals when they commemorated their victories and triumphs." This statement applies to the other races as well as to the Incas, but Garcilaso adds a touch of local color that at once brings in the human element. He says that "There were (in 1560) five Indians residing in Cuzco, who were great masters on the flute, and could play readily by book any tune that was laid before them." This is an indication that the Indians had learned to read musical notation during the time that the Spaniards had been in the country. Garcilaso continues that the five Indians belonged to one Juan Rodriguez, who lived at a village called Labos, not far from the city. "And now at this time it is reported (Being the year 1602) that the Indians are so well improved in musick, that it is a common thing for a man to sound divers kinds of instruments."

The accounts differ as to their voices, some saying that they were sweet and others, harsh, but Garcilaso liked the voices of the half-breeds. Father Acosta says, "They did all sing and dance to the measure of these instruments with so goodly an order and accord, both of their feet and voices, that it was a pleasant thing to behold." Father Sahagún (1499 (?)-1590) seems to have found both good and bad singers, as one might naturally expect, and in the following quotation, one seems to hear him struggling with the difficulties of a choir of Indian neophytes. He says that "The good singer has a clear, true, good voice, a good mind and a good memory, and whether he is singing tenor or low, softens and tempers his voice. He leads for the others and occupies himself with composition and teaching and he practices before appearing in public. Whereas, the bad singer has a rough, harsh voice, and is violent and untutored, presumptuous, immodest and jealous. He molests and annoys the others, and is forgetful and avaricious. He does not wish to pass on

ceremony will often have a tonal and structural pattern belonging only to that ceremony and not to be otherwise used.

to others what he knows, and he is proud and *muy loco.*" (Very crazy.) Father Sahagún laments that at first the natives seemed to follow the teaching of the friars but later grew distrustful, and "now they sing and dance and make their holidays when and where they please, and they sing the old chants that they had in the time of idolatry—and no one understands what they say because the songs are very veiled."

As is the case among many peoples in the earlier stages of civilization, the professional poet and minstrel were often one and the same person. They composed lyric, dramatic and war-like poetry, and often used it for dramatic festivals. Scholars describe their compositions as having vivid imagination, and ample vocabulary and say that they all loved nicety of expression; the Nahuatl enjoyed flowing periods and the Mayas, sententious brevity. Unfortunately, of the compositions only a few still remain. Garcilaso has preserved the words of one whose subject is an old Peruvian tradition;—A maiden of royal blood is appointed by the creator to pour water and snow on the earth out of a pitcher. Her brother breaks the pitcher, whereupon thunder and lightning arise.[7]

Of Mexican poetry before the days of the Spaniards, we have accounts from several sources, notably through the efforts of one of the early friars, Bernardino de Sahagún, who wrote down seventy-

---

[7] Philip Means made a free verse translation of this lyric as follows: (See Ancient Civilization of the Andes P. 435).

> Beautiful princess,
> thy dear brother
> thy cup
> is now breaking.
> So for this
> there is thunder,
> Lightning,
> thunderbolts falling.
> But, princess,
> thy water,
> dropping, rains
> where sometimes also
> there will be hail,
> there will be snow.
> The maker of the earth,
> Pachacamac
> Viracocha
> for this duty
> has placed thee,
> has created thee.

See also Tschudi, Travels in Peru, 1838-1842, D Bogue, London.

nine *Cantares Mexicanos,* in the *Nahuatl* language. These have been translated into Spanish and republished in facsimile as well.[8]

They have been described as graceful poems in rhythmic prose. They are not simple couplets as their Spanish name, *Cantares,* might imply, but long pantheistic poems, and they were sung for both priestly and secular festivals. It is a matter of record that for thirty years after the conquest they were still sung. During that time they had changed in character to wails or complaints about the oppressed condition of their singers and thus incurred the disapproval of both the civil and religious authorities.[9] They were then stopped.

One of the *Cantares* is the greeting of Nezahualcoyotl on visiting the aged Moctezuma in Mexico when he was ill, and begins as follows:—

"1. Most estimable and august Spirit, see how I come to you, lean and whitened as a yellowing flower. I come from Acolhuan where beautiful flowers flourish.

2. Listen to these my songs with which I come to gladden you, Oh! Sovereign Moctezuma, with my royal plume of emerald green which is the honorable custom."

This is only the opening, but it gives an impression of the ornamented style. Unfortunately we know of no music connected with it.

Some of the *Cantares* make dignified and beautiful appeal to the "Dispenser of Life;" all of them use flowers, birds, light and mountains in their symbolism.

At festivals and ceremonies the dance was generally joined with music. All writers are unanimous in describing as extraordinary the skill of the natives in dancing. Their accounts help to shed light on the music. The following is taken from Clavigero,[10]

"However imperfect they were in music, their dances in which they exercised themselves from childhood, under the direction of the priests, were most graceful. They were of various kinds, and were differently named, according to the nature of the dance, or the circumstances of the festival for which they were made. They danced sometimes in a circle, and sometimes in ranks. At some dances only

---

[8] Don Mariano Rojas, Don Antonio Peñafiel.
[9] El folklore y la musica Mexicana. R. M. Campos, pp. 14-15.
[10] History, Vol. 2. pp. 208 et seq.

men, and at others only women danced. On such occasions, the nobles put on their most pompous dresses, adorned themselves with bracelets, earrings, and various pendants of gold, jewels, and fine feathers, and carried in one hand a shield covered with the most beautiful plumes, or a fan made of feathers; and in the other an *Ajacaxtli,* which is a certain little vessel which we shall mention hereafter, resembling a helmet, round or oval in shape, having many little holes, and containing a number of little stones which they shook together, accompanying the sound, which is not disagreeable, with their musical instruments. The populace disguised themselves, (see illustration p. 4) under various figures of animals, in dresses made of paper, or feathers, or skins.

"The little dance, which was made in the palaces for the amusement of the lords, or in the temples, as a particular act of devotion, or in private houses, when they celebrated nuptials, or made any other domestic rejoicings, consisted of but a few dancers, who formed themselves in two parallel lines, dancing toward the other extremity of their lines; sometimes the persons of one line faced those correspondent to them in the other. Sometimes one of each line detaching themselves from the rest, danced in the space between both, while the others stood still." (See illustration.) This illustration, of Peruvian origin, shows the dancers in a row, as does Clavigero's description of the Mexican ceremony. The comment of the Spanish writer, Lopez de Gomara, was that it was a grand thing to see, and that he liked it better than similar things to be seen elsewhere.

Clavigero describes what he calls the "great dance" of the temple, and says that it was performed in large open spaces of ground, or in the area of the greater temple, and differed from the little dance in the order, form, and number of the dancers. Some hundreds of people used to join in this dance. The music was placed in the middle of the area or space; near to it the lords danced, forming two, three, or more circles, according to the number of them present. At a little distance from them were formed other circles, of dancers of less rank; and at a small interval from them, other circles proportionately larger were formed, which were composed of youths. All these circles had for their centre the *Huehuetl* and the *Teponaztli* (the two kinds of drums.)

This made a figure shaped like a wheel, the spokes of which

TRUMPET PLAYER AND CONCH PLAYER FROM A GOLD PLAQUE

FIGURE 1

FIGURE 2

PLATE I. DECORATIONS FROM ANCIENT PERUVIAN TERRA COTTA VESSELS

DANCERS WITH INSTRUMENTS AND MASKS
Photographs by courtesy of the American Museum of Natural History,
New York City

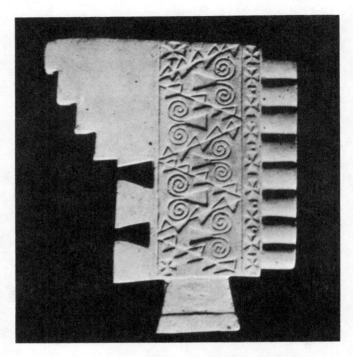

ANCIENT CARVED STONE PANPIPES FROM PERU

FLUTES, MADE OF BONE, SHOWING VARYING NUMBERS OF HOLES

consisted of as many men as the innermost circle of nobles. "All the dancers described a circle in their dancing, and no person departed from the radius or line to which he belonged. Those who danced close to the music, moved with slowness and gravity, as the circle which they had to make was smaller, and on that account it was the place of the lords and nobles most advanced in age; but those who occupied the station most distant from the music, moved with the utmost velocity, that they might neither lose the direction of the line to which they belonged, nor the measure in which the lords danced."

Lopez de Gomara, in his *Historia de México,* gives a long description of ceremonial dancing, which was preceded by the grave and slow singing of ballads, probably the account of heroic doings. But as the Indians became more aroused they sang joyous songs and the dance waked up and became very intense. Acosta's account is that "They did all sing and dance to the sound and measure of their instruments, with so goodly an order and accord, both of their feet and voices, and it was a pleasant thing to behold."

In the festivals that combined singing with dancing, the singing often was an alternation between a solo phrase and one from the whole chorus. There would be buffoons dancing in the space between the lines of dancers, who would disguise themselves in strange clothes or animal costumes, and excite the mirth of the whole gathering. When one set of dancers was exhausted, another would take its place, and in that way they managed to keep going for many hours. This is still the case with the modern Indian celebrations.

The older historians always seem to have stressed the human sacrifices among the various American races, without much stress on the element that made the psychological under-current,—that is, effort to appease deities who had the power of injury toward the life of the whole tribe. The modern scholar Joyce * concludes that undoubtedly human sacrifice, while prevalent, was not as frequent as the chroniclers implied. Clavigero says that the prisoners who were to be sacrificed "spent the preceding night singing and dancing with the temple attendants and others."

He also describes a curious dance which suggests the familiar

_____

* See **Mexican Archaeology"**, Chap. 3, also Joyce's other writings.

Maypole dances of our ancestors, and is still kept up by the people of Yucatan.[11]

"They fix in the earth a tree or strong post, fifteen or twenty feet high, from the top of which, according to the number of dancers, they suspended twenty or more small cords, all long and of different colors. When each dancer had taken hold of the end of his cord they all began to dance to the sound of musical instruments, crossing each other with great dexterity until they formed a beautiful network of cords round the tree, on which the colors appeared chequered in admirable order." (See illustration p. 14.)

On some of these occasions the musicians were in the center with the dancers around them, and at other times the musicians were hidden. Father Salvatierra found that some of the dances imitated the efforts involved in hunting and fishing, or the harvesting of roots or fruits. Many of the dances had nothing licentious about them, and at least one, according to Torquemada, was so solemn, so beautiful, and so fitting that it was admitted into the Christian temples. This dance was named the *Tocotin* or *Tocontin*. Thomas Gage says that it was danced before the King of Spain, by persons who had learned it in the Indies. Father Salvatierra further tells us that he had counted as many as thirty different dances, some sacred, some war dances, and others of festival character. In 1649 Alonzo de Ovalle wrote this description; "Their way of dancing is with little jumps, and a step or two, not rising much from the ground, and without any capers such as the Spanish use. They dance all together in a ring."

The ceremonies of court life, both in Peru and Mexico, had their musical accompaniment, and we hear on one occasion that "Nezahualcoyotl made his musicians sing, to the accompaniment of various instruments, an ode which he had composed himself. It had for it's subject a comparison between the shortness of life and its pleasures, and the fleeting bloom of a flower." Bernal Diaz de Castillo describes Moctezuma's banquets at which were present what we would call jesters and minstrels. According to other reports, the instruments on these occasions were flutes, bells, shells, bones, and timbrels. Royal weddings and births were also excellent occasions

---

[11] For descriptions of Maypole dances see, "The Golden Bough, 1 vol, Edition MacMillan 1922, Chaps. 9 and 10. A similar dance is still in use.

for music. In Peru there were certain recognized forms of vassalage, and among others, the Indians of a certain district were evidently considered as especially good dancers, for it was their responsibility or privilege to supply performers for the court.

Funerals of important chiefs gave a fine opportunity for impressive ceremonials, and the body was carried to the temple in solemn procession. The priests came first with braziers of copal, singing melancholy funeral hymns, which were accompanied by the "hoarse and lugubrious sound of flutes." [12]

Both in Peru and Mexico when the ruler went forth in state, some of the nobles preceded him with garlands of flowers, dancing and playing on musical instruments and preparing resting places for him in the fields. This must have been a general custom, for the missionary Huldericke Schmidel, who was in the La Plata river country between 1534 and 1554, describes the same kind of ceremony. He says that they had instruments resembling the crooked trumpets called *schalmes* in Europe. Schmidel also speaks of music at mealtimes among the chiefs in that part of the world. He says, speaking of the ruler himself. "He is wont to have music at table and at meat, whenever he pleaseth. For then they play upon the flutes of pipes, men leading the dances and skipping with most beautiful women, which dances and skippings seemed so strange to us, that looking upon them, we had almost forgot ourselves."

Father Acosta is equally vivid in describing the music and dancing in the temple ceremonies, when he says—[13] "then came forth one of the chiefs of the temple, attired like to the idol, carrying flowers in his hand, and a flute of earth, having a very sharp sound, and turning toward the east he sounded it, and then looking to the west, north and south, he did the like—during which ten days the priest did sound this flute." A further description of Acosta's, which confirms the statements of other writers of the period, is the following, "In these dances they use sundry sorts of instruments, some of which are like flutes or little flutes, others like drums, and others like shells; but commonly they all sing with the voice, and first one or two sing the song, then all the rest answer them. Some of these songs were wittily composed, containing histories, and

---

[12] "De Solis, History of Mexico, 1691."
[13] Natural and Moral History of the Indies, P. 378 Hakluyt Ed.

others were full of superstitions, and some were mere follies." He describes a Peruvian feast in which, with their bodies ceremonially painted, and hung with golden ornaments, they cast flowers on the highway; and then "they all did sing." Finally, Acosta sums up his impressions that nowhere in the world was "such a curiositie of playes and dances as in New Spain where at this day we see Indians so excellent dancers as is admirable."

The ceremonies described in this chapter come close to dramatic representation, and among the various Indian races comedy and tragedy were both used, and diverting masquerades were widely popular. Acosta says, "We have not discovered any nation of the Indians, that live in communities, which have not their recreations in plays, dances and exercises of pleasure. In Peru I have seen plays in manner of combats—. In these dances they use sundry sorts of flutes or little canons, others like drums and others like cornets, but commonly they sing all with the voice.—They have likewise put our compositions of music into their language, as Octaves, Songs and Rondels, which they have very aptly tuned." The names of some of these plays or dramas have reached us, and one or two copies of dramas written down by the Spaniards, as the Peruvian *Ollanta* or *Ollantay*,[14] the Kiché "Rabinal Achi", and Popol Vuh and the Books of Chilam Balam of Central America. In such cases it is difficult to be certain just what is Spanish and what Indian, but the traditional element in these dramas antedate the time of the Spaniards.

There are various descriptions of performances witnessed by the early settlers and missionaries, with a stage decorated with branches and flowers, feathers and fruits all picturesquely arranged. The actors presented comic or even farcical scenes, in which they pretended to have all sorts of bodily defects, for the relief of which they prayed to their deities. "The deaf answered those who spoke to them with cock and bull stories, the lame with acrobatic feats." All this was done in ways that excited the risibilities of the audience. Acosta says, "These buffoons were succeeded by others who represented animals, one was a beetle, another a toad, a third a crocodile, and so on. . . . These animals discoursed among themselves, explained the parts they played upon earth, and each of them claimed to be

---

[14] For further exposition and scholarly discussion see **Ancient Civilizations of the Andes** by Philip A. Means, pp. 440, et. seq.

TWO CEREMONIES
With trumpets, conch shells, drums, flutes, rattles. The little footprints indicate the pattern of the dance. See Clavigero's description of what he calls a Maypole dance. From the Codex Bornicus

WHISTLING JAR
By kind permission of E. Weyhe from Fuhrman's Reich der Inka

the first." Similar shows are still to be seen occasionally in remote parts of the country. The actors showed great skill in their performance we are told, and they in turn were followed by the pupils of the seminaries, who imitated birds and butterflies, and roosted in the trees, where the priests pelted them with pellets of earth, and meanwhile gave them comic advice.

The existence of so many kinds of ceremonial music is an indication that a primitive art was in process of developing, with a type of ceremonial music that was more than just a spontaneous folk expression, and for which some kind of training was considered necessary. So it is not surprising to find that there were schools in Mexico, Yucatan and Peru for perpetuating the musical traditions, and to these institutions the important members of the community sent their children.[15] The training and discipline were rigid. But we find also that the children were joyful and given to play, and that in their play they were so friendly, that "there is no bad name heard nor any scurrility." From the musical standpoint their voices were considered worthy of care, for the girls were warned not to talk or sing through their noses.

Closely connected with the question of teaching, was the matter of recording the national annals, of which the singing has been described a few pages back. These records were kept partly by the Elders or Wise Men, and partly by the minstrels. In the Inca tongue the former were called *Amauta,* while in the Aztec language the name was *Nahualli.* The minstrels selected the most vivid incidents for their songs or ballads, which were sung on festal occasions. Even in the mythology of early Peru, there was a hero-deity, who had a special trumpeter, a man who played on certain great shells much esteemed by the Indians.[16]

Ciéza de Léon describes these compositions as the recital of the great events in the history of the race, which could in this way be kept before the people. They were to be sung only on great occasions, and one form of punishment for unworthy monarchs was that their record was omitted, thus condemning them to well-merited oblivion, while the good rulers had their fame preserved. After

[15] See article by Auguste Genin, Smithsonian Report, Sept. 1920, pp. 657-8.

[16] See P. A. Means, **Ancient Civilizations of the Andes,** Quotation from Father Cabello. 1576-86.

the death of a monarch, the scholars and minstrels would be called and given their directions. These Elders and Wise Men are reported to have had in many cases remarkable memories, sound judgment and great reasoning powers.

So far our accounts refer to the mainland of South or Central America and Mexico. But contacts were also being made with the Islands of the Caribbean and the Philippines, so there are a few available reports about these regions. The same conditions apply generally here as on the mainland; ceremonies, festivals, the same tirelessness in singing and dancing, an alternation between a solo voice and a chorus, and a union of song and dance. Las Casas especially liked the music of the Siboneyes, the indigenous natives of Cuba.

In the case of the Philippines, the reports leave one in doubt as to whether the available information refers to truly indigenous conditions or to conditions that grew up after the arrival of the Europeans. But there were boisterous festivals that lasted often as long as a week.[17] The dancers formed a circle with arms extended, and hopped alternately on one foot and then on the other, sticking the raised foot out behind, meanwhile uttering terrifying shrieks; and all to the noise of a big conical drum. They played on their drums with their hands; here we are reminded of the description of the natives of the Americas drumming with their fingertips. The drums described are of types also to be found in India and the Moslem countries.

Among the men with Magellan on that first adventurous journey around the globe, was an Italian named Pigafetta, who described landing in Cebú in April 1521. They had many negotiations with the natives, among whom they found a variety of instruments of different kinds, including brass gongs made in China. They saw young men playing on pipes similar to those used in Portugal. They had the good fortune to see a dance in honor of the sun, in which some old women alternately blew on bamboo trumpets and danced and shouted. Pigafetta was conducted to the royal residence by the son-in-law of the chief, where they found four youths playing on instruments, the first a drum similar to Portuguese drums. Next

---

[17] See pamphlet by M. Walls y Merino, La Música popular de las Filipinas.

was a kind of drum played with palm-wood sticks, and lastly cymbals which were very sweet in tone and well played. He also described a type of rustic flute, and an instrument which he calls a viola. In Kroeber's book, there is a description of a similar instrument, made of a joint of bamboo from which several cords of the surface fibre had been slit except at the ends. These cords were then given a tension by being elevated on a bridge.

One of the early accounts of Philippine music adds a touch of unconscious humor to a subject otherwise solemnly treated, for in speaking of their devotion to song, music and dance, it says that "the first was monotonous, the instrument of reeds, and the dance pantomimic." This writer could not have had the instincts of the anthropologist or folklorist, or he would certainly have found an endless variety of further facts with which to embroider his tale. Fortunately for us, some of the early writers are more observing and more sympathetic.

The fragmentary quotations given in this chapter make a picture that is incomplete but still shows considerable line and color. The most serious gap is that the actual tunes are lacking. The nearest that we can come to these is among the melodies of the Indians who are still primitive today, the *Indios Bravos*.

Chapter Two

THE FUSION—THE COLONIAL PERIOD

INTO this aggregation of races and cultures came the Spaniards with their varied antecedents, and at a very high pitch of their racial vigor. They had by this time finished driving out the Moors, with whom the eight centuries of contact had been of inestimable worth. But behind that lay their own background which was "the product of original stock; the Romans trained this stock and gave it their language and civilization; the Visigoths brought their Teutonic usages; Arabs and Moors communicated their manners, their modes of life;" and the Spanish nation came into being.[1]

Items about the beginnings of Spanish musical history are unfortunately sparse but a few are available before the time of the Moorish invasion, for it is recorded that on the completion of the Roman conquest, shortly before the commencement of the Christian era, a group of Iberian prisoners was paraded in the triumphal procession, and impressed the Romans highly with their music. Later, in the fifth century, there was a Queen in Portugal, named Cindasunda, who was a great patroness of the art of music. Whether we should call it real music or not, is another question, but the old recorder was much affected.

Catholic Church music takes a place in the records of this period, for some of the Spanish prelates, notably one of the Bishops of Toledo tried to eliminate from the music used in the ritual, the various and extraneous elements which had crept in. Thus we get a glimpse, however faint, of activities in both secular and religious music. Taken all together these musical activities made a sturdy stock for later development, and when the Moors and Arabs came in 706 A. D., their music found fertile soil in which to grow.

---

[1] This vivid characterization is by H. D. Sedgwick in his introduction to *A Short History of Spain*.

The earliest traces of music in Asia Minor and the Arabian Peninsula take us back to the third Millenium B. C.[2] according to the latest scholarship. Occasional fragments of information carry us along through the days of Babylon and Assyria to the time of Muhammad. Then more data becomes available, for Muhammad himself is said to have disapproved of music as beneath the consideration of serious minded men, but the whole question of the early Islamic attitude toward music is one on which scholars disagree. Suffice it to say that after the death of Muhammad in 632 A. D. his followers over-ran Persia and Byzantium, and as they liked the music of both those countries adopted it for their own. Back in their own country, the music developed during the course of the next three or four generations into a vigorous art, primarily vocal in character, but including a variety of instruments, and taking elements from both Persian and Byzantine sources. It reached it's culmination during the reign of Harun Al-Rashid, 786-809 A. D., and the first one or two caliphs who followed him.[3] It was during Harun's time that one of the most talented and distinguished musicians of his court, called Zyriab, departed for Spain because of the jealousies he encountered among the other court musicians. Thus it came about that the best of the oriental tradition was carried westward by a man so gifted in every way, that he was able to set fashions in the music of the day, which by degrees became an integral part both of the folk-music and the sophisticated music of Spain. Fortunately the fusion of these elements was not only a matter of palace life, where whims of fashion reign in music as in other things, but took root in the hearts of the people, who preserved it and made it grow.

The Moors kept their foothold in southern Spain more surely and for a longer period of time than in the north, so the music of the south has always had more oriental flavor, and that of the north, a color more like the rest of Europe. Thus Spain has in many ways a closer spiritual bond with North Africa than with Northern Europe. The north-west corner of the country, including Asturias and Galicia was the region least touched by the Moors and was the retreat of the Christian Government for many years.

[2] History of Music in Arabia, H. G. Farmer.
[3] See **The Music of Ancient Arabia and Spain**, Chap. 9, pp. 19. Ribera-Hague.

The entire period until the time of the discovery of America was one of steady development in music. During the early part of the fifteenth century the Gypsies are first heard of in the Spanish peninsula, where they settled principally in the southern part. At first little is known of their doings, except that laws of extraordinary severity were passed against them, so their misdeeds must have been many. Andalusia, in the south, is the region which shows most strongly their influence in music. As many of the early settlers of the new world came from the coastal districts of that part of the country, they carried with them undoubtedly much of the oriental flavor of Gypsy music which was being diffused around Spain.

By the sixteenth century Spanish music had reached a splendid height, and in many ways was ahead of Northern Europe, musically. The lute was the important instrument in secular music, but various others of wood and metal were also used, as well as different members of the viol family, both plucked and bowed. The sophisticated art of the upper classes was beautiful, and involved a very considerable technique, as may be seen by examining the books of lute music or the old song books. The contemporaneous popular and folk-music of the time was to be heard everywhere and all the time, according to the writers of the day, and included fascinating songs and dances.[4] The Church music had much inspiration and skill expended on it, and the best of the Spanish composers like Tomas Luis de Victoria ranked with Palestrina and his followers in Italy.

Spain was a land of many beautiful, heroic ballads, *romances* as they are called in Spanish. They had grown up during the middle ages and had become very much a part of the daily life of the people. The earliest collections do not include any music, which appears first in the song collections of the sixteenth century. By the time of the conquest of America they were sung and recited and known by heart by a large portion of the population, to such an extent that more than one sophisticated Spanish writer speaks of them disparagingly and refuses to quote them because of their commonness.

That the ballads were among the earliest importations into the new world is shown by a fragment from the *conquistador* Bernal Diaz de Castillo. He describes sitting about a camp fire somewhere in the

---

[4] See **The Music of Ancient Arabia and Spain.** Chaps. 9 & 10.

wilderness with a group of soldiers, and says that an entire conversation was carried on among the group by means of one quotation
after another from these ballads, flung across the fire quickly and
vividly by these often unlettered men.

There are many evidences that ballads were not the only music
imported by the first comers. Many of these early settlers came from
the maritime districts of Southern Spain and brought with them
their southern speech with it's Moorish elements and none of the
lisp of Castile. They also brought the songs of their region which
are always strongly imbued with local color. This fact accounts for
many sudden reminiscences of the Orient that come to light unex-
pectedly in Spanish America, in their music and also in their customs of living. An old document lists the soldiers, sailors, artisans
and workmen of various sorts who made up the quota of one flock
of early settlers, and specifically mentions two musicians who were
brought "to make gayety for the populace." Another old document
tells of a group of musicians who came from Seville, two or three
violin players, and two or three fife players. Most of them could sing,
and they were engaged to play at local fiestas, "receiving pay therefore and a ration of wine, and transportation." It is recorded that
Cortez took some musicians with him when he set out to conquer
Central America.

There must have been various adventurous musicians among
the soldiers of Cortez, and we hear of one named Ortiz, a "Tocador
de *bihuela,* y enseñaba, a danzar." That is, he was a player on the
bihuela, which was one of the predecessors of the guitar, and also a
teacher of dancing. In 1525 this man started a school for dancing
in Mexico City for "the embellishment of the city." A school for
church music was inaugurated at about the same time by Fray
Pedro de Gante (Ghent), the first to be started in the western
hemisphere by Europeans, in contrast to those of the natives which
we have previously mentioned. As music was a necessary part of
the church ritual, the fathers began training their Indian neophytes
and found them as a rule gifted and willing. The presence of Spanish schools shows that the cultural development of the country was
going on in various ways. So we find that the first printing-press was
introduced into Mexico City in 1536 or 7, but printing was for a
long time an expensive luxury, not to be entered into lightly. Many

of the early books were religious, with a goodly proportion devoted to church music.

What might be called a census was taken in Mexico City in 1574, which showed that the city had a well-built Spanish quarter, with churches, monasteries, university and other schools, besides the two mentioned in the preceding paragraph. There were also four hospitals, of which one was for Indians. This is still in existence. There were workmen's guilds, each settled in their own district. The instrument-makers had a special guild and many of the members were Indians who became extremely skillful at their trade. There were organs in all the convents and churches, and many uses for instruments of different kinds in secular music, and it is quite obvious that such instruments did not all come from Spain. For secular use guitars, *bihuelas,* harps, *rabels* and so on, were all customary.

Meanwhile Central and South America were both developing along these same lines, although in point of time, often somewhat later. The archives of Caracas show that Venezuela had a school for plain-song as early as 1591. By that time Lima also had correspondingly important public buildings and schools. All these items go to show the impress made by the Spaniards on the life of the new continent. It is well for those of us who live in the United States of North America to remember a few comparative dates, for our history may almost be said to begin with Jamestown in 1607, the Mayflower in 1620, Massachusetts Bay in 1630, and Maryland in 1634. Even then, it was sometime before we had rich cities with all the organization described here.

The Spanish-American colonial period may be divided into two parts in a general way. During the first, the amalgamation was going on between Spanish and Indian, or Portuguese and Indian, with the additional element in certain parts, of the Negro slaves. This lasted till the end of the eighteenth century. Thereafter the welding process was further complicated by the addition of settlers from other parts of Europe. But of that, more will be said later.

So far, we have only touched on the happier side of the beginnings of Spanish colonial life; but the meeting of Indian and European was far from smooth, nor is the relationship completely stabilized even today. It took time to acquire even a moderately comfortable working basis. The main outlines are a matter of history, and

are all tied up with the incredibly difficult task that Spain under-
took when she started to colonize a continent so many times her own
size and with such uncounted hordes of primitive inhabitants. In
making an estimate of her accomplishment one must not forget
that the point of view of even the most intelligent and advanced
thinker of that time could not dominate his century.

The Missionaries of the various brotherhoods, Jesuits, Dominicans, and so on, were among the early comers, and, besides teaching them, did much at times towards alleviating the hard lot of the
Indians all over the continent. Missions grew up in many out of the
way corners, and we hear of individual missionaries as far afield as
the upper reaches of the Amazon country and the La Plata River
country in the latter part of the sixteenth century.

The Padres were ingenious about taking all opportunities to
extend their influence, and Alfred Maudslay has found one case in
Guatemala that interests us because it shows the spread of Spanish
music among the less civilized tribes. He says that [5] "the method
adopted by the Dominican missionaries to overcome the hostility and
suspicion of the fierce inhabitants of Tuzulutlan, and to gain the
confidence of their chiefs was simple and ingenious. Las Casas and
his three brethern, Rodrigo de Ladrada, Pedro de Angulo and Luis
Cancer, had all acquired a knowledge of the Quiché language,
dialects of which were spoken both in Guatemala and Tuzulutlan,
and in this language they composed verses embodying the story of
the fall of man and his redemption, and the other tenets of the
Christian faith. They then sought out four Indian traders who were
accustomed to make journeys to Sacapulas and Tuzulutlan to sell
their goods, and to these men, who had already become Christians,
the Padres taught the verses they had composed, so that they might
chant them to the accompaniment of native instruments and the
tinkling of little Spanish bells. Small articles of European manufacture for presents to the chiefs were added to the trader's packs,
and they set out for Sacapulas, where they were well received by its
cacique, who was then by far the most influential man in that part
of the country. When the trading was over for the day and whilst
the chief persons in the neighborhood were still assembled in the
house of the *cacique,* the traders begged the loan of some musical

5 "A Glimpse at Guatemala." pp. 96-7.

instruments and then, tinkling the *"cascabeles,"* which they had brought with them from Guatemala, they commenced their chant.

The novel form of the music and the wonderful story which the verses told, had the wished-for effect on the hearers, so that the chant had to be repeated time after time and day after day, to increasing crowds of eager listeners. When however, the *cacique* inquired more closely into the meaning of the words of the song, the traders told him that they themselves were unable to give him any further explanation, as that could be given by the padres alone. "And who then are these padres?" asked the *cacique,* "for I have never seen or heard of them." The traders replied that they were men clad in black and white garments, who wore their hair cut in the form of a wreath, who ate no meat, and who desired neither gold nor cloaks, nor feathers nor cacao, who were not married yet lived chaste lives, who sang the praises of God both day and night, and possessed beautiful images, before which they knelt in prayer, and that these alone could explain the meaning of the verses; but that such good men were they, and so ready to impart their knowledge to all, that should the *cacique* send for them they would most willingly come to instruct him. The *cacique* pondered over the words of the traders, and finally agreed that his younger brother, a youth of twenty-two years, should accompany the traders on their return journey to Guatemala. He privately instructed the youth to seize every opportunity to learn if it were really true that the Padres possessed neither gold nor silver, and did not beg for it nor hunt for it, as all other Christians did, and whether it were true that they neither had women in their houses nor treated with them elsewhere. It is needless to say that the young Indian chieftain was well received at Guatemala by Las Casas and his companions, and that he returned to his country well pleased, in company with Luis Cancer, who successfully commenced the conversion of the people."

It was an easy step for the Indians in all the missions to move on from their own temple ceremonies and dramatic representations, to the religious performances instituted by the Padres. These were called *auto sacramentales*. The Padres used the natural talents of their flocks to present religious drama, for this could be made of great assistance to their teaching. As a rule the subjects were taken from the scriptures, though sometimes the conflicts between the

Christians and Moors were presented. Brinton says that at times the more intelligent natives were even permitted to write the texts. Such performances are still given in our day, and have incidental music with them; so it is fair to infer, considering the emotional value of music, that it would have been used at that earlier period.

The Jesuits developed their missions in Paraguay in very early times, and ran them as a kind of benevolent despotism in contrast to the merciless tyranny of the conquistadores. They saw to it that their Indian neophytes' tasks were made as attractive as possible, and so always had a little band of music; and the workers sang on the way out to the fields in the morning and returning in the evening. An excellent musician, Father Juan Basso was brought from Europe, especially to teach music and singing to the *Guarany* Indians. Father Basso must have found life in the missions quite a contrast to teaching music in an archducal school in Europe.

Meanwhile the Portuguese were opening up Brazil, and at the time of discovery (about 1500) the Indians found there, the *Guarany,* were in a far more primitive state than the races we described in the first chapter. They had not learned the use of metals, neither do we find monuments to their ability in building, like the extraordinary examples found further north. The Portuguese came, as did the Spaniards, at the apex of their national strength, when they excelled not only in physical prowess, but in literary and artistic ways as well. Three native ethnic elements are included in Brazilian life, for Negro slavery was introduced in the early days of the colony. As there was much race mixture, the Indian, the Portuguese, and the Negro strains go to make up the hybrid.[6] In music, the results show even up to the present day, for the types of song and the rhythms are different from those found elsewhere. We shall go into the details in the chapter on music.

During the whole colonial period, the New World was full of excitement and romance for enterprising spirits who came over from Europe. One of the most vivid of these who has recounted his experiences, was an Irishman named Thomas Gage, who spent a number of years in Mexico and Central America, during the first quarter of the 17th century.[7] He was brought up as a priest in a

[6] **La Literatura Argentina.** Buenos Aires. 1917.
[7] **A New Survey of the West Indies.** London. 1648.

monastery at Valladolid in Spain, and like many other young men of the time, was fired with eagerness to help christianize the Indians. His descriptions of what he saw around him are colorful and even spicy. He was much impressed by the wealth of Mexico City, and says that the streets were broad enough for three coaches to go abreast in the narrowest, and six in the widest, and that there were fifteen thousand of them in the city." He adds a by-word of the day, "Four things are fair, the women, the apparel, the horses and the streets," and continues, "and the beauty of the coaches, which do exceed in cost the best of the court of Madrid, and other parts of Christendom, for they spare no silver nor gold nor precious stones, nor cloth of gold nor the best of silk from China to enrich them." In one place he comments on the fact that everybody is well-dressed, even the slaves and blackamores.

As a friar it is natural that Gage should be especially interested in telling about the churches, monasteries, and convents, and their music. He sounds a complaint which has rather a modern tone to it, for he stresses the fact that people went to church for the music rather than "the service of God."

This failing was true of other countries as well as Mexico. He particularly mentions the excellence of the music in some of the churches in Guatemala, with inferences as to the size of the congregation. He records that in the Guatemalan churches, "The Fiscal or clerk must be one who can read and write, and he is commonly the master of music—On the Lord's day and on other Saint's days—in the morning, he and the other musicians at the sound of the bell, are bound to come to church to sing and officiate at Mass, which in many towns they perform with organs and other musical instruments—and at evening at five o'clock—they again resort to the church when the bell calleth to sing prayers."

Gage has much to say about music in the convents, and describes the musical competition between nunneries, also that music was considered so important, that girls with good voices but no money could often get into the most luxurious of the convents. An insight into this luxury is reached by the description of a Guatemalan lady of high rank, Doña Juana de Maldonado y Paz, who "was the wonder of all that cloister, yea, of all the city, for her excellent voice and skill in musick—and for her ingenious and sudden verses—. In her closet she had a small organ, and many sorts of musical instruments, whereupon she played sometimes herself, sometimes with her best friends of the nuns, and here she entertained— the bishop."

The Jesuits, says Gage, petitioned the King to allow them the privilege of teaching the Indians; among other things "to perfect them in musick and all musical instruments." Gage describes at length fiestas which he saw in different localities, and the customs and music that went with them. They included sacred plays, well performed by the Indians, many times under the direction of the Jesuits, and sometimes involving many months of preparation.[8]

So far we have dealt with Mexico and Guatemala, but there were festivals in other places as well. One is reported from Lima, in the early part of the seventeenth century, in connection with the canonization of Saint Ignatius Loyola. There was intense enthusiasm in the streets and churches and monasteries, so that the air was full of the sound of pealing bells and "the music of clarinets and other instruments." In the evening a grand *Te Deum* was chanted, and the Dominicans came in a procession. Vast numbers of people who had originally come from the Basque country in Spain, of which the Saint was a native, made a special celebration with music and fireworks.

Festivals were not always purely religious, for a contemporaneous Chilean fiesta included three days of bullfights as a commencement and then three days of plays and interludes interspersed with dancing of several sorts and religious ceremonies as well. On this occasion the orchestra consisted of a harp and some guitars. Where such fiestas were frequented by many natives they were apt to end wildly, but before they grew too riotous they must have been extraordinarily picturesque, for strange costumes and strange music were the order of the day. Even such sad occasions as carrying of the Host to dying people came into this category, for in some places it was carried in a gilded coach, followed by a small orchestra consisting of a variety of instruments, listed on one occasion in the Mexican town of Oaxaca as the double basses, violins and guitars, and other instruments. Meanwhile the church bell was sounded gently.

Even today, Spanish America is a country of strong contrasts,

_____
[8] Ibid. pp. 154-5.

at one extreme highly civilized cities, with everything that goes to make a well-developed culture, and at the other, the remote ranch country and virgin back-country with some of the most primitive tribes to be found anywhere in the world. In colonial times such contrasts were if possible even stronger than today. In the eighteenth century Bishop San Alberto reported to his superiors on the impossibility of keeping up the church services in the remote districts, for lack of towns or villages to which to draw people, lack of priests, churches and all that was needed for the ritual, not to mention the lack of communications between ranches. Another writer states that the type of man desirable for the priesthood was so scarce that one had to be satisfied with what one could get. A quaint human document of a little later date, 1670-1709 is in the form of an old note book with manuscript entries of various kinds, local, historical, astronomical, etc., with occasional songs interspersed. The book belonged, during those years, to a Friar dwelling in the region near Cuzco in a Franciscan monastery. He was a Spaniard named Gregorio de Zuola, and was the preaching Friar of the organization. Life was evidently lonely on the Andean plateau and he must have had many attacks of nostalgia for what he had left behind in Spain, as evidenced by some of the songs and some of the other entries. The jumble of scattered notes and songs is also mute testimony of the value of paper and scarcity of books.

Since Friar Gregorio's day the book has belonged to a number of people and is now in the hands of that most worth while scholar, Ricardo Rojas of Buenos Aires. It has been studied and deciphered by Carlos Vega, one of the musicians of Buenos Aires.[9] Such a picaure is hard to believe in our day; it was, and still is, true of vast stretches of back country. But, on the other hand such conditions made the best kind of soil for folk-songs to grow in. Needless to say, they did.

The families of white origin who lived on ranches buried in the wilderness, had great difficulty in carrying out their religious observances. They had no choice but to make use of some man or

[9] There are seventeen songs in all,—one a Credo, while the others make quite a characteristic cross-section of Spanish music of the day, things which he, the lonely monk, might easily have remembered, and tried to retain, for festival occasions. They are melodious simple tunes, some ballads, some love songs, and some choral numbers.

woman on the ranch who could act as lay-reader or what might be called deacon or deaconess. For important ceremonial days he or she would learn the liturgic text in Spanish or Latin, so that the ceremonies might be piously carried through, often including hymns and chants. The person who officiated in this way took on an importance in the life of the ranch only to be equalled by that other important member of remote communities, the one who was skilled in nursing and the use of herbs.

In these far-off regions the inhabitants greatly simplified their music as well as their few instruments, usually employing only those that were easily portable, although in the better type of manor house there were apt to be quite a variety of instruments and even books of music. Some of the hymns or chants were the compositions of local priests and grew into the traditions of the district almost in the same way as did the secular folk-music. The little tunes (p. 37) are taken from a book published in 1717, and while no clue is given as to their origin, might easily have been from such a source. Songs or hymns to be sung in the early dawn before starting out to work were a general institution, and were called *alboradas*. These are still to be heard in the country, as well as the songs that are intended to be sung in the evening around the fire. Until most recently there have been places where one might still find professional mourners or wailers for funeral ceremonies. This is reminiscent both of the primitive Americans and of the Moorish background of the Spaniards.

The eighteenth century was a time of literary and musical sterility throughout Spanish-America, although the folk-music went cheerfully on its way. In contrast to the common folk and their music, are the accounts of the sophisticated life going on at the vice-regal courts. These people led very artificial lives which aped the pomps of court life in Europe. The customs of the day included many dramatic representations given by the members of the courts with much scribbling of verses and making of little tunes to go with them. There is a delightful old description of the Count of Revillagigedo in Mexico in 1752, giving a fiesta with music and dancing and a banquet at his country estate at San Angel outside of Mexico City. There are other similar accounts from Lima and other South American cities. But among the upper classes in all these countries there was a fashion for copying Italian models, in opera especially, and therefore in lyric music as well. The Italian influence was really a detriment here as elsewhere, for it led Spanish American music into channels that were not natural to it, and therefore not entirely sincere. Later again, came a fashion for copying French models, or others, all of which resulted in an equally ungenuine product. But these passed in time. We find one interesting item of Mexico City in 1786 about the "Teatro Coliseo". The records show that the orchestra of the Coliseo theatre included five violins, one violincello and double bass, two oboes and two trumpets. A document of the time states that Miguel Gálvez played the cello, was to teach two *piezas* every month, repair the worn out music, and *suplir al contrabajo*. José Mariano Ortega was made a member of the orchestra, to play the violin and act as messenger to the other members for getting them together. Luis Degreso was second flute, and expected to substitute as second trumpet, *bajo octavino* or to play the *clarin* on occasion.

During the eighteenth century the Spanish colonial enterprise spread in a north-westerly direction into the region which later became California, Arizona and New Mexico, and this story is so much better known to those of us who live within the boundaries of the United States that there is no need to dwell long on this phase of the subject. The country grew up first through its missions and presidios, then followed vast ranches, and lastly the large cities. Life was somewhat easier in California than in the region further east, because of climate, and because even in early days it was more accessible by water. But conditions throughout the whole stretch were such as to be favorable to the good development of folk-music; that is, there was always an innate fondness among the inhabitants for singing and dancing, and their diversions were home-made in the sense of not depending on external elements. Because of their separation from the rest of the world these qualities developed to an especial degree.

We find that in Spanish California balls were given in the plaza or public square, or in large arbors, with hard level earth floors, and hung around with sheets, coverlets, etc., to keep out the weather; that the orchestra was apt to consist of two violins and a guitar; that for wedding celebrations the festivities lasted often for as many as three days, with dancing and feasting and singing.

Endless books of travel, both old and new have been written about Spanish America; and it is interesting to note in how many cases the writer's own psychology comes to the surface. When we read the accounts of the more impressionable writers, we gain an excellent composite picture of the importance of music in the lives of the colonists. But among other writers a longing for the roast beef of Old England or real German sauerkraut or other such non-essentials loom up and their books are worthless for this type of study.

At the beginning of the eighteenth century, according to the more reliable of these writers, there was hospitality to be found beneath every roof, whether simple or luxurious, and a welcome with it. There was singing and dancing among the Indians, the mestizos, and the Europeans. Teachers were few and far between, so the music was usually of simple kinds, with simple, locally made instruments, but natural talent was very general. For the well-to-do-woman, music was practically the only diversion, and her children, her house and her religion bounded her world. One scribe reports that among the women of Maracaibo the favorite instrument was the harp, although usually in other places it was the guitar; but women's lives in general so restricted, must have been greatly enriched by music.

A writer tells us that the fiestas in Caracas began with *Novenas* in the churches, followed by public amusements, such as fireworks, concerts, balls and church processions with much music, in which were carried statues of various saints dressed in gorgeously decorated garments. In a letter from Bogotá, in the early part of the XIX century, we read that after an "evening party the guests went home on foot at about one o'clock, in the moonlight, and singing local songs." Among the lower classes we find that gatherings lasted all night, and that towards morning they were apt to acquire a more savage character, and the songs became more licentious. But there are comparatively few instances reported of intoxication or riotous behavior, whether that is because everybody expected drunkenness and riotousness, I leave to the reader.

The following description is from Captain Basil Hall, an Englishman who skirted much of the South American coastline in his ship. He was hospitably received wherever he went, and his account gives an excellent cross section of the life of the times. He describes a festival of Negro slaves in Panama in the moonlit center of an open grass square, about which some sat while others danced in great circles. The music was nothing if not primitive, a cocoanut shell struck with a short stick. When they all joined in the singing it was loud but not discordant. He also frequented the best society, which he describes with evident sympathy and pleasure. In Chile, he writes of going "to the house of a neighbor, an old lady, whose great delight was to see her friends happy about her. We were soon joined by several other families, and there being a pianoforte in the room, the sure consequence was a dance.—It is quite impossible to describe the Spanish country dance, which bears no resemblance to anything in England. It consists of a great variety of complicated figures, affording infinite opportunities for the display of grace, and for showing elegance of figure to the greatest advantage. It is danced to waltz tunes, played in rather slow time; and instead of one or two couples dancing at once, the whole of the set, from end to end, is in motion. No dance can be more beautiful to look at, or more bewitching to be engaged in; yet there is no denying, that admirable though it be for these warm regions, it is of a character unsuited to the climate and habits of England. This is one of the few times in which Captain Hall allows himself to become insular.

The following description, also by Hall, refers to one of his stops on the Pacific Coast of South America. The picture is cheerful, after a gloomy introduction. "We dismounted at the door and were shown into a bleak, comfortless room with a mud floor, a rude unfinished roof, lighted by a solitary black tallow candle, all of which made us feel instinctively sure of a cold reception. In this, however, we were much mistaken, for the master of the house no sooner saw who we were, than he begged us to walk into his sala or drawing-room, a very different apartment from the first, for as we entered, we could scarcely stand the glare of light from a dozen wax candles. The floor was covered with a rich carpet, the roof and cornices were neatly finished, and the walls ornamented with mirrors and pictures. At the upper end of the room stood a grand pianoforte, by Broadwood, and at the tea table near it, the lady of the house and her daughters received us most kindly. We soon became acquainted; and while one of the young ladies went out to gather some flowers for us another opened the pianoforte and played very good-naturedly while we were chatting with the old people."

The intermediate, middle-class entertainment in all the countries did not involve elaborate, special invitations. There was always a guitar in the offing, which was in frequent use either for dancing or accompaniments for singing. Many times there would be people present who could extemporize verses in honor of distinguished guests.

The instruments most in use by the first half of the XIX century, among the well-to-do, were, as we have seen, pianos, harps, and guitars, and it is interesting to note that though pianos were sometimes of European manufacture, laboriously imported into the new country, yet there were piano factories in Pernambuco, Brazil, and Durango, Mexico, as early as the first part of the nineteenth century. One traveller states that 1840 was the date of importation of the first piano to Tegucigalpa and that was followed soon by others (not Broadwoods or Erards). He says that they had to be carried two hundred and forty miles on *human* backs from the coast. By the time they reached their destination they were considered as worth ninety to one hundred pounds. Guitars were nearly ubiquitous among both rich and poor. Guitar technique was sometimes carried to a high degree of perfection, so one may read of performances of Haydn and Bach on the guitar that sound like the beautiful art of our contemporary Andres Segovia. Home-made fiddles were common enough. Various types of harp were in use. One was laid across the knees instead of being used upright. Sometimes the role of singer and instrumentalist was delegated to two individuals, but more often not. Improvisation was almost a fine art and cultivated by many. The dancing among the better classes was graceful, with complicated figures which afforded good opportunities for skill and elegance. Usually the country dancing was better than that in the cities. Travellers give similar accounts of different sections of the country, so such tales as the foregoing may be taken as generally characteristic.

The Argentine country was the setting, all through the middle of the nineteenth century, for a type of folk-singer who has grown into enduring face. *Gaucho* was the name for the cattle ranchers and cowboys on the Pampas, and the Gaucho combined in his temper-

ament many of the qualities of his Castilian ancestors, as well as of
the hispanicised Arab and the Indian. In repose, he was dignified,
low-voiced, with few gestures, but capable of fierce passions when
angry; but he had a strong sense of honor, and he was generous and
hospitable to a fault. His life made for love of adventure, melancholy,
fatalism, and above all individualism. He was an essentially religious being, but rebellious of forms and ceremonies. The life was a
lonely one and conducive to song. The *Payador,* as the singer was
popularly known, was one who could accompany himself on the
guitar, and who could improvise in eight syllable lines, accounts of
local events. Into these ballad-like compositions he would intersperse
his own comments and philosophising. His style combined a certain
epic quality, and a Moorish sadness, lightened by a touch of real
Andalusian wit, and made a type of music that was rich in emotional
expression and far from primitive. His songs were the logical descendants of those of the minstrel or troubadour in Europe, and also
of the long dramatic or historical ballads of the aborigines. They
were also the predecessors of the later types of songs, *Vidala* or
Vidalita, Cielo, Cielito, Triste, Serenata and so on. The Gaucho
loved to express his idea either veiled in mysticism or superstition or
else with an element of malice or sentitentiousness, according to the
scholar Ventura B. Lynch. The songs were full of feeling for the
open country, and the unfettered, horseback life of the wilderness.
Likewise, the dances; for when the Gaucho particularly wished to
show off his skill it was the *Malambo* that he chose. At times they
had contests which often lasted for days. During his existence, the
Gauchos singer was an important and vital figure in the land.

Some of these men grew famous as individuals, so that their
names have come down to us. Santos Vega was a real Gaucho *payador,* but became almost legendary after his death. He was the idol
of all gatherings in the La Plata and the Salado districts, a wanderer
always welcomed wherever he stopped, and unrivaled in his minstrelsy: till finally there came a day when someone else outsang
him, and the legend was current for a long time, that the conqueror's
guitar strings sparkled with flames and that a red light shone around
him. Santos Vega could not face defeat, so he disappeared, never to
return.

Hilario Ascasubi, also a noted *Payador,* came somewhat later and made many of his songs under the name of Paulino Lucero. Under this assumed name he grew to have mythical attributes. Another *Payador* rose to fame as a general of Gaucho troops, for whom he composed *vidalitas* to sing on the march so as to help them forget their weariness. The story goes that the tyrant Rosas was in the habit of attending gatherings of the common people and of having *payadores* present, who would sing laudatory ballads about the tyrant's own exploits. Such songs were often barbaric in subject matter and expression. Toward the end of the century the inspiration for this kind of music with its characteristic verse was waning, but not before it had influenced extensively the currents of later music. Even today in places like the Sertão district of Brazil there are minstrels who follow the old traditions of minstrelsy, and are the logical descendants of the men of the middle ages. In the chapter on music we shall refer to this influence again.

During the period of the *payadores* in Argentina, the native fondness for music continued to grow all over the country and to fill a great need in the lives of the people. We are fortunate to be able to find details which show the currents in other countries as well. Life in and around Mexico City had a gifted and charming analyst at this time in Mme. Calderon de la Barca, the Scottish wife of the first Ambassador to be sent from Spain to Mexico after the break between the two countries. Naturally she was in a peculiarly favorable position for seeing and hearing music of all kinds. She went to all the big state functions, and noted the fashion for Italian music there and at the opera. The performances must have been excellent, and most picturesque as well, for all the local nobility went attired in their handsomest brocades and laces, mantillas and combs and other finery. Moreover, she wrote of the audience as decidedly musical. She liked the music that she heard in private houses, and even though competent teachers were lacking, she says that they managed to make delightful music.

Mme. Calderon de la Barca lived in Mexico long enough to be present at the church ceremonies of the whole year, and at these she heard much music. Of one occasion she says that "The church was superbly decorated and only well-dressed people admitted." This remark carries its own deductions. She goes on, "The music was beautiful but too gay for a church. There were violins and wind in-

DELL'HISTORIE DEL

furono fatti ſoggetti da gl'Ingui, comandarono che ogni vno imparaſſe la lingua del Cuſco, & che i padri la inſegnaſſero a i lor figliuoli. Coſi queſto linguaggio generalmente s'uſa per tutti quei paeſi che loro ſignoreggiauano.

Come gl'Indiani del Peru adorano il Sole, & lo tengono per il ſuo principal Iddio.

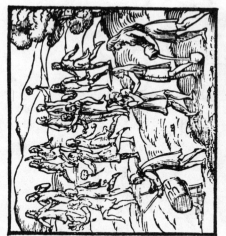

Queſte genti ancor che parlano col demonio, tengono per loro principale Iddio il Sole, & quando no-gliono

SUN WORSHIP IN PERU

DELL'HISTORIE DEL

ballare minore : & ballano in queſto modo.

Modo di ballare.

Si vniſcono inſieme dugento, e trecento, & ancora tre, & quattro mila, conforme alla Prouincia doue ſono genti aſſai o poca, & nettato beniſſimamente la piazza doue hanno da ballare, vno di loro paſſa auanti a guidare la danza, andando quaſi ſempre indrieto, riuolgendoſi qualche volte, & coſi tutti

A DANCE WITH DRUMMER IN THE FOREGROUND
From Historia del Mondo Nuovo, G. Benzoni

Both photographs by courtesy of the H. E. Huntington Library, San Marino

Ma-ri-a, todo es Ma-ri—a, *Mary, all is Mary,*

Ma-ri-a, to-do es à vos: *Mary, all is yours:*

Toda la noche y el di—a *All the Day and Night*

Se me vai enpenfar en vos. *I think on nothing but you.*

2.
Toda vos refplandeccis *You are all glittering*
Con foberano arrebol, *With Sovereign Light,*
Y vueftra cafa en el Sol *And David fays*
Dice David que tencis. *Your Houfe is in the Sun.*

HYMN TO THE VIRGIN MARY

Zapateo, a
Dance in Pe-
ru and Chili.

DANCE TUNE
Both from F. R. J. de Pons A Voyage to the Eastern Part of South America.
Both photographs by courtesy of the H. E. Huntington Library, San Marino

struments and several amateur players. Some pieces from the *Cheval de Bronze* were very well played.[10]

Mme. Calderon de la Barca's descriptions of the various church festivals are vivid enough to be quoted in her own words;—"We are now approaching the holy week once more—in Mexico a scene of variety in the streets and of splendour in the churches; but in the country a play, a sort of melodrama, in which the sufferings, death, and burial of our Saviour are represented by living figures in pantomine."

"The first evening we arrived here (San Angel) there was a representation of the Pharisees searching for Christ. The Pharisees were very finely dressed, either in scarlet stuff and gold, or in green and silver, with helmets and feathers, mounted upon horses which are taught to dance and rear to the sound of music, so that upon the whole they looked like performers at Astley's. They came on with music, riding up the lane until they arrived in front of this house, which being the principal place hereabouts, they came to first, and where the Indian workmen and servants were all collected to see them. They rode about for some time, as if in search of Christ, until a full-length figure of the Saviour appeared dressed in purple robes, carried on a platform by four men, and guarded on all sides by soldiers. It is singular, that after all there is nothing ridiculous in these exhibitions; on the contrary, something rather terrible. In the first place, the music is good, which would hardly be the case in any but a Mexican village; the dresses are really rich, the gold all real, and the whole has the effect of confusing the imagination into the belief of its being a true scene."

"The next evening the same procession passed, with some additions, always accompanied by a crowd of Indians from the villages, men, women, and children. Bonfires were made before the door of the hacienda, which were lighted whenever the distant music was heard approaching, and all the figures in the procession carried lighted lamps. The Saviour was then led up to the door, and all the crowd went up to kiss his feet. The figure which is carried about this evening is called "Our Saviour of the Column," and represents

[10] **Life in Mexico. First Edition, P. 232.**
I have not been able to trace this name, but it was probably that of some Operetta.

the Saviour tied to a pillar, bleeding, and crowned with thorns. All this must sound very profane, but the people are so quiet, seem so devout, and so much in earnest, that it appears much less so than you would believe.

Christmas time of course means lovely celebrations of which the following descriptions give a good idea;—"In the evening we went to the house of the Marquesa de V—o, to spend Christmas Eve. On this night all the relations and intimate friends of each family assemble in the house of the head of the clan, a real gathering, and in the present case to the number of fifty or sixty persons.

"This is the last night of what are called *Posadas,* a curious mixture of religion and amusement, but extremely pretty. The meaning is this: At the time that the decree went forth from Caesar Augustus, that "all the world should be taxed," the Virgin and Joseph having come out of Galilee to Judea to be inscribed for the taxation, found Bethlehem so full of people, who had arrived from all parts of the world, that they wandered about for nine days, without finding admittance in any house or tavern, and on the ninth day took shelter in a manger, where the Saviour was born. For eight days this wandering of the Holy Family to the different *Posadas* is represented, and seems more intended for an amusement to the children than anything serious. We went to the Marquesa's at eight o'clock, and about nine the ceremony commenced. A lighted taper was put into the hand of each lady, and a procession was formed, two by two, which marched all through the house, the corridors and walls of which were all decorated with evergreens and lamps, the whole party singing the Litanies. K—walked with the Dowager Marquesa; and a group of little children, dressed as angels, joined the procession. They wore little robes of silver or gold lama, plumes of white feathers, and a profusion of fine diamonds and pearls, in *bandeaux,* brooches, and necklaces, white gauze wings, and white satin shoes, embroidered in gold.

"At last the procession drew up before a door, and a shower of fireworks was sent flying over our heads, I suppose to represent the descent of the angels; for a group of ladies appeared, dressed to represent the shepherds who watched their flocks by night upon the plains of Bethlehem. Then voices, supposed to be those of Mary and Joseph, struck up a hymn, in which they begged for admittance, saying that the night was cold and dark, that the wind blew hard, and that they prayed for a night's shelter. A chorus of voices from within refused admittance. Again those without entreated shelter, and at length declared that she at the door who thus wandered in the night, and had not where to lay her head, was the Queen of Heaven! At this name the doors were thrown wide open, and the Holy Family entered singing. The scene within was very pretty; a *nacimiento*. Platforms, going all round the room, were covered with moss, on which were disposed groups of wax figures, generally representing passages from different parts of the New Testament, though sometimes they begin with Adam and Eve in Paradise. There was the Annunciation—the salutation of Mary to Elizabeth—the Wise Men of the East—the Shepherds—the Flight intto Egypt. There were green trees and fruit trees, and little fountains that cast up fairy columns of water, and flocks of sheep, and a little cradle in which lay the infant Christ. One of the angels held a waxen baby in her arms. The whole was lighted very brilliantly, and ornamented with flowers and garlands. A padre took the baby from the angel, and placed it in the cradle, and the posada was completed." [11]

Later she says that the rustic voices were fine in the *Ora pro nobis*. "But music in this country is a sixth sense. It was but a few days before leaving Mexico, that sitting alone at the open window, enjoying the short twilight, I heard a sound of distant music; many voices singing in parts and coming gradually nearer. It sounded beautifully and exactly in unison with the hour and the scene. At first I concluded it to be a religious procession; but it was not a hymn, the air was gayer. When the voices came under the window, and rose in full cadence, I went out on the balcony to see to whom they belonged. It was the *forçats* (prisoners), returning from their work to the Acordada, guarded by soldiers, their chains clanking in measure to the melody, and accompanied by some miserable looking women." At least the poor prisoners had a way of lightening their weariness.

tice but now they are recognized as belonging in the class of folk

Singing in the street leads one naturally to street cries, and Mexico City must have had a generous share of these. In former times such things as street cries were considered as unworthy of no-

[11] **Life in Mexico. PP. 238-239.**

expression. Mme. Calderon de la Barca tells us that "There are an extraordinary number of street cries in Mexico, which begin at dawn and continue till night, performed by hundreds of discordant voices, and impossible to understand at first. Señor — has been giving me an explanation of them, until I begin to have some idea of their meaning. At dawn you are awakened by the shrill and desponding cry of the *carbonero,* the coalman, "Carbon! Señor," which as he pronounces it, sounds like "Carbosiu!" Then the grease-man takes up the song, "Mantequilla! lard, lard, at one real and a half." Salt beef! good salt beef!" (Cecina Buena), interrupts the butcher in a hoarse voice. "Hay cebo-o-o-o-o?" This is the prolonged and melancholy note of the woman who buys kitchen-stuff, and stops before the door. Then passes the *cambista,* a sort of Indian she-trader or exchanger, who sings out, "*Tecojotes por venas de chile?*" a small fruit which she proposes exchanging for hot peppers. No harm in that."

"A kind of ambulating peddler drowns the shrill treble of the Indian cry. He calls aloud upon the public to buy needles, pins, thimbles, shirt-buttons, tape, cotton-balls, small mirrors, etc. He enters the house and is quickly surrounded by the women, young and old, offering him the tenth part of what he asks, and which after much haggling he accepts. Behind him stands the Indian with his tempting baskets of fruit, of which he calls out all the names till the cook or housekeeper can resist no longer, and putting her head over the balustrade calls him up with his bananas and oranges and granaditas, etc."

Mme. Calderon de la Barca's experiences in Mexico date from the Forties of the last century, but for most of the period thereafter until the present time her descriptions keep their value as representative of the life to be found there. It is only comparatively lately that the processes of evolution are really evident and that changes are visible.

Meanwhile in the Philippines, the development was somewhat different from that in the western hemisphere, because of the close contact with Asia, and the differing circumstances of climate and insular conditions. The musical instruments show the nearness to Asia, for Chinese gongs are much used instead of bells. There are also Oriental variants of some of the other instruments, both among the stringed group and the wind. Similarities are to be found in the uses for music; open air church festivals with music included, likewise fiestas near the manor houses, also religious drama with music. The Islands have been an especially fertile field for the preservation of the old ballads and the creation of later ones. They have been a real part of the life of the people so that till the present time, conversation has often been sprinkled with apt quotations from the well-known ballads; while modern ballads, known as *corridos* are still growing up about interesting events. There are various collections of such, both old and modern, usually giving just the words, for the would-be performer is expected to know the tunes. This is a present-day continuation of the *Broadsides* of former times in Europe.

As we reach the latter part of the nineteenth century there is an ever increasing number of available accounts of South and Central American music, as described by people who have heard it. The travellers always return with reports of the excellence of all that was to be heard in the way of amateur singing, and the charming simple home evenings with music and dancing among the middle classes. The fondness for drama was universal where drama was to be had at all, and where legitimate drama was difficult of accomplishment, puppet shows were resorted to with the local band for orchestra. Naturally, the band would play more or less local music that the audience could recognize and enjoy. We find descriptions from various regions, one by Alfred Maudslay in his book on Guatemala. He describes festivals in which the dancing lasted all night, with the dance called *Zapateado* often predominating. He also says that one could usually tell where a *Fandango* was going on, and speaks of the "men who grow active and excited, and echo the passionate dancing of Spain, while the women are graceful but slow in movement, with downcast eyes, as though to mark the Indian side of the mixed blood." Such festivals always meant that "there would be music, not only by the strolling *marimba* player who inevitably turns up at all fairs and festivals, but by an orchestra of harp, violin, guitar and guitarilla, for the Indians of Vera Paz are a musical people, and they play original tunes to which the traditional dances are performed. The names of these dances were "Deer and Hounds," "The Monkey Dance," "Death Dance," or "the Moros and Cristianos." The dances were performed with becoming gravity by untiring young bucks, whilst inside the house, before the saint, the *Zon* [12] would be solemnly gone through with by the older people."

Ruben M. Campos in his excellent book, *El folklore y la música mexicana,* has recorded the names of various of the singers and guitarists and other musicians of local fame, whose music, like Stephen Foster's in the United States, has become part of the folk inheritance of Mexico. They were often born and bred in little remote villages with small opportunity for school training. But they had the gift of lyric melody and as a rule, agreeable voices; to which they usually added a good guitar technique. With this equipment they went around the country from one local festival to the next, singing songs of their own composition as well as the current songs of the day, much as the troubadours of the Middle Ages did throughout Europe. Nowhere in the world does the performer find a more willing audience. Their own compositions were melodious enough to be caught by the listeners and spread hither and yon over the country-side. Cheaply printed sheets of the words, like the old *Broadsides* and those we have spoken of previously, helped in the popularization of these songs, and hand organs followed suit. Later the phonograph did its share also. Wandering minstrels, in groups of two or three or singly, made a hand to mouth existence going from fair to fair, and also helped to keep going the continual flow of this type of simple melodious music.

One of the best known of these musicians, Antonio Zúñiga, lived in a small town in the state of Guanajuato, Mexico. He gained international fame, through the influence of two German musicians who heard his songs when they travelled through the country and carried them to Berlin. There they created a real furore, as this episode happened before the present interest in all sorts of folk-music. Many of Zúñiga's songs have been lost as they were not written down and published at the time of composition. A man of similar attributes in Brazil was named Gregorio de Mattos, a very gifted and prolific writer of *modinhas.*

Another case of musicianship of similar type is to be found in a family named Júarez in Mexico, in which the combined group, father and sons make up a small chamber orchestra, consisting of violin, cello, or double bass and clarinet. The cellist is the composer

---

[12] Zon was the name given to a dance considered to be the especial prerogative of the older people.

of the family but all of them have a natural gift for counterpoint, and their playing is masterly.

There are villages in which groups of men or girls, or both, make up organizations, and give really creditable performances. In the winter of 1910, the writer ran across a group of wind instrument players at a little village festival in the mountains. They were of the peon class and wore the universal white cotton clothes. From some remote hamlet further back in the mountains, they had come down with the intention of playing some of their little tunes in front of the church, on the afternoon of the fiesta. They stood on the steps of the building, their whole attitude one of the most profound devotion, and went through their simple repertory, as though performing a sacred ceremony, while the market was going noisily along outside the enclosure, and the village boys set off fireworks in broad daylight from the church roof.

Another experience during the same year was in the town of Oaxaca, where lived at that time a big six-foot man, a nearly full-blooded Indian who was a real example of the folk musician. For all his cotton clothes he had the manners of the proverbial Spanish grandee, and he was an artist in his own way. His specialty was to clamp a mouth organ on to the upper side of his enormous guitar, and with the former he would play a melody and its' second, stooping over his larger instrument to reach the mouth organ, while he made his one guitar sound almost like a small orchestra as he played the accompaniment on it. In Brazil, there is a singer of the folk musician type named Patricio Texeira, a negro, with an agreeable natural voice and some training, who has gained a wide reputation in his own specialty.

This type of folk musician is in direct contrast to the men or women who have been brought up in the usual traditions of northern European music. The latter are increasing in number, dwelling mainly in the larger centers, where a more international culture flourishes. Their work is often of high standard and has reached European shores sooner than our own, which is our loss. We shall speak further of them in the last chapter.

Chapter Three

THE LAST TONAL FRONTIER—LOS INDIOS BRAVOS

Modern Aztec Love song from the Sierra of Tamaulipas in Mexico
I know not whether thou hast been absent,
I lie down with thee, I rise up with thee,
In my dreams thou art with me.
If my ear drops tremble in my ears,
I know it is thou moving within my heart.
                    D. G. BRINTON, *Essays of an Americanist*

THE extreme contrast between the sophisticated life in the cities and the primitive life in the remote country regions of Spanish America has already been stressed. We have also followed the fusion of Spaniard and Indian during colonial times; but certain tribes resisted the hybridizing process more than others, and thus have remained in more or less savage state, or with only slight alternations in their customs. Throughout the whole colonial period these Indians have been pushed further and further back into the wilderness, the mountain Indians ever further into the recesses of the Andes, and their jungle brethren deeper into the jungle. Some tribes have entirely disappeared, for they stood no chance against the superior war materials of those who were forcing them backward. It is almost impossible to estimate the number of those who remain, and it would be quite unfair to imply that all the tribes that do still remain could be classed under a general heading of savages. There are many shades of difference between those with or without vestiges of former indigenous culture, or those who have adopted a detail here and there from the lives of the Spaniards who happen to be nearest to them. Musically, however, these differences are slight and can be stated in a somewhat general way.

According to the admissions of various scholars, less is known about the untamed Indians during the colonial period than about

the more advanced races during the pre-Columbian times. This is
due to the fact that the early contacts between Spaniards and Indians were mainly with the more advanced races. There are a few
exceptions however, for the reports of Father Fritz and of Father Ul-
rich Schmidel, both dating from the middle of the sixteenth century
and describe conditions in the wilds of the river country of South
America; but the most important to us is the account given by a
Frenchman named Jean Léry or in its' latinized form, Lerius. The
first edition of the book is in Latin and was published in 1556 and
republished in 1590. He travelled through the wilds of Brazil and
tells of the sights he saw with such understanding and such pains-
taking care that he deserves to be considered as the forerunner of
the modern folklorists, although his findings might not stand the
acid test of modern methods. He describes the ceremonies and in-
vocations that took place before fishing or hunting expeditions, to
propitiate the fish or animal deities, and actually took down the little
tunes which he heard the natives sing. Whether or not these render-
ings were phonographically correct is not so important as their early
date, and the similarity which they show to the familiar types of
tunes found among other primitive Indians.

Léry describes a festival as follows. The wording and old
spelling is taken from an old translation.

"All the men went into a certaine cottage, the women into another, and the children also into a third.—The Caraibes, before they
departed from the women and children, with great care forbad the
women to go out of their cottages, but diligently to attend to the
singing—. We heard a low, soft muttering noise breaking out of the
house into which the men had severed themselves, (for that cottage
was almost thirty paces distant from ours.) The women were about
two hundred in number, standing and giving ears, gather themselves as it were on an heape. But the men, lifting up their voices
little by little, so that their distinct words were heard of us, exhorting and likewise repeating this interjection—.[1]

Pira- ouaſſou a-ouch, Camou roupou y- ouaſſou a-ouch.

---

[1] Theodore Roosevelt in his "Through the Brazilian Wilderness", gives
a similar description, pp. 200-201, 219. Another suggests the following of
Lerius.

Léry goes on to say that, "they heard the women presently with a trembling voice singing the same interjection again. *He, he, he,* etc. And they lifted up their voices with so great vehemency of minde, and that for the space of one whole quarter of an hour, that they drew us who were the beholders into admiration. And surely they did not only horribly howle, but also leaped forward with great violence.—

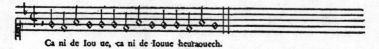

Ca ni de Iou ue, ca ni de Iouue heuraouech.

"At length these cries ended, the men being somewhat silent, the women and children also holding their peace, presently the men bgan to sing so sweetly and with so great harmonie, that I was wonderfully desirous of seeing them." [2]

Lerius is one of the few writers who distinguishes between sweet singing and harsh on the part of the Indians. He goes on to describe the ceremonies still further and says that they lasted for two hours with the men continually dancing and singing. What he calls the tunable singing was so sweet, he says, "that to the unskillful it is scarcely credible how excellently well that harmonie agreed, especially seeing the barbarians are utterly ignorant of the art of musicke. And surely, although in the beginning I was stricken with a certaine feare, as I lately mentioned, yet contrarily then I was so much overjoyed, that I was not only ravished out of myself, but also now, as I remember the tunable agreement of many voices, both my mind rejoiceth, also mine eares seem continually to ring therewith, but especially the burden of the song yielded a pleasing sound unto the eares, which at the end of every verse they sang after this manner:

Heu, heura, heura, etc." [3]

The Indians finished by stamping vigorously and shaking the right foot with violence; then they all spat and all shouted the closing phrase, He, He, hua.

Léry then begged the interpreter to explain the things he had not understood and was told that the commencement was a lament for their valiant ancestors. They continued by taking comfort in the

[2] **Purchas his Pilgrimes.** John Lerius, Vol. XVI. pp. 553, 554. (See illustration P. ?) Translation.
[3] Idem, vol. XVI. pp. 556, 557.

fact that after death they would join them beyond the mountains, and there dance and celebrate with them. Next they threatened their enemies, and after that sang about a flood that had happened in the past.

One other writer of the sixteenth century, Father Hulderike Schmidel, in an account of the music at the court of a savage ruler in mid-South America, tells of ceremonies suggestive of these described in the first chapter, as happening among the Aztecs and Incas. Lionel Wafer, who lived among the Indians of the Isthmus of Panama for four months, during the year 1681, writes of their music. He says that they had a musical director or master of ceremonies called *camoturo* who was an important official. "In this favorite dance, called the *guayacan,* the *camoturo* plays upon the *camo,* a kind of flute made of a piece of *caña-brava*. The men and women form a ring about the player, beat the floor twice with the foot and advance two steps, when they break the chain and the couples come together and revolve rapidly in time with the music." Wafer also speaks of shell trumpets for war music, and drums.

In the eighteenth century, Father Dobrizhoffer gives two little items that are worth recording. He says that the subjects of the songs were warlike expeditions, the despoiling of the enemy, the capture of towns and depopulating of Spanish settlements. These descriptions were not "rudely made", but with considerable elegance. Dobrizhoffer also says that the singers performed two at a time and that when once they get started, it was hard for them to stop. "One of the women standing apart from the men, signifies, by percussion of her lips, to the performers after about fifteen minutes that it is time for them to stop and give the next group a chance."

To find further accounts of customs among the less civilized Indians, written with equal sympathy, intelligence, and observation, one has to seek among writers much closer to modern times. All these later writers from 1850 onwards describe certain customs which one grows to recognize as fundamental, as belonging to all American Indians, but they give also many local details which are the results of regional conditions.

The Indian is often described as a somber, taciturn creature, as if still dreaming of ancient power and of many wrongs suffered. D. H. Lawrence says of the Mexicans that they have a "strange and

VIEDVS wer sandt von der Wildtnußk der Jndianer Religion vnnd Gottesdienst ...

vero eorum adeo suauis erat, vt inexpertis vix sit credibile, quam optime sym-
phonia illa quadret, praesertim cum Barbari musicae artis penitus sint ignari. Ac

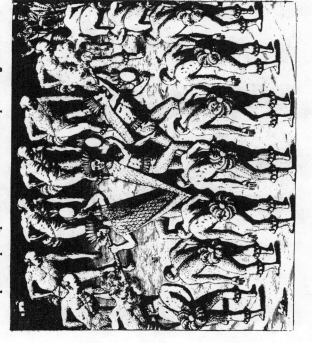

CEREMONY BEFORE AN IDOL

With flute, drums, masks, Bry. 16th century

Courtesy of the H. E. Huntington Library, San Marino

CEREMONIAL DANCE ACCORDING TO DE BRY

FESTIVAL AT GUAQUI, BOLIVIA
Photographed by
Dr. Robert Hegner of
Johns Hopkins University

mysterious gentleness between a Scylla or Charybdis of violence."
The Indian keeps the memories of his great heroes and their deeds
even till the present time, as well as many customs that go back to
pre-Spanish times. Phillip Means closes his extremely scholarly work
on the ancient civilizations of the Andes with the following para-
graphs, "Years of observant wandering and diligent study have con-
vinced me that of all the ancient and still surviving people none is
more tenacious of its past, and none more likely—under favorable
circumstances—to surprise the world some day with a splendid
renascence of its former genius, than is the venerable native stock
which today comprises more than half the Andean population. In
spite of all the evils that have weighed upon them for four centuries their spirits are not crushed.—"

He goes on to say "that the hidden fires of artistic and political
fervor still burn within the breasts of this oppressed, this miserable, this despised race. Mocked at for dullards, gulled for var-
lets fit only for the ox's toil, defended—when defended at all—only
by the soap-tongued politician—the indigenes of the Andean region
are indeed in a tragic plight. Not until true understanding of their
genius, of their requirements, and of their practical worth is won,
will they come into their own, and in the ingredients of that understanding the materials provided by archaeology will constitute the
major part." To that last statement one might add that the understanding of their arts will be an additional bond.

The Christian religion has as a rule been super-imposed on the
Indians' earlier beliefs but has done little more than dent the surface. Some students believe that the principal change has been to
substitute semi-theatrical performances for old ones that were ob-
scene or brutal, but that these modifications do not hide the indigenous elements. On the whole, although the condition of the Indians
cannot be said to be any too good, the consensus of opinion among
writers quoted in this book, is that it is better now than it was in
colonial times.

The Indigenes still talk their own language and sometimes
Spanish as well. Their customs show the results of contact with
the Europeans in varying degrees, sometimes as in the upper reaches of the Amazon, almost nil. In Paraguay for instance, the Indians
still talk *Guarany,* and often it will be only the upper classes that

talk Spanish. In the Andes, *Aymará* and *Quechua* are still living languages, and in parts of Mexico there are still remnants of *Nahuatl,* to give just a few examples.

In their music, the Indians are partial to tunes based on a five tone scale,[4] although this is not constant. As with the Pre-Columbian Indians, the scales on which their tunes are built are often influenced by their primitive instruments. A case in point is the music of the *Alacalufe* Indians of southern Chile, in which the five notes would be more nearly represented by 1 2 3 5 flat 7 than the usual 1 2 3 5 6. Of course the Indians' own mental approach is far from being as theoretic as the foregoing statements might appear to indicate. At times a variety of other scales are used, more nearly resembling our modern major and minor, and are probably the result of contact with the Europeans. The instruments are thoroughly simple among the backward Indians, and include all that have come down to them from their ancestors, drums, flutes, rattles, shell trumpets, also panpipes of many sizes. They enjoy tying bells around their knees or ankles when they dance.

Their tunes are mournful and full of melancholy, with fine vigorous rhythms. Many villages boast their own orchestras, sometimes even two kinds of orchestras. One is made up of the older men with the traditional instruments, and is called on for ceremonial occasions, when the traditional music is needed. The other is drawn from those inhabitants who have had more city contacts, and have come back to their native heath with city instruments and tunes and dances. This latter type presages the breakdown of the older, more characteristic music, and often offers no other substitute than jazz. One difference between these two types of organization is that the older men in playing their ritual music, hold strictly to the conventions, while the other group is more apt to change with whims and impulses, and feels free to employ its fondness for improvisation.

Before the days of the Spaniards, dancing was considered as a form of worship, as we have shown. Even now many tribes of Indians still consider it as such, and the dance alternates with periods

---

[4] For collections of songs based on a five tone scale, see M. Béclard D'Harcourt, Melodies Populaires Indiennes, and La musique des Incas et ses survivances. Also Cancionero Incaico, V. G. Cáceres. Pub. by the Instituto de Literatura Argentina, Buenos Aires, Argentina.

of kneeling and praying before the altar of whatever saint is being celebrated. Bandelier describes dances that took place in the Andes Mountains, because of the fear caused by an eclipse of the sun or the moon, others because of drouth. The same statement holds good for other parts of the continent. Again, the Indians danced because their burial places were disturbed, or to placate evil spirits, at which time they also played their flutes. In some parts of Peru the people make a festival of shearing the lambs and dance during the celebration. In Panama, the Indians have a special hymn to be sung when the mangoes are in flower, which implores the benediction of the Good Spirit. In all parts of the continent dances are performed before the shrine of some special saint, to prevent or cure illness, or in the celebration of puberty rites; or again to ward off danger or after escape from danger. There are still to be found dances in honor of the sun, or to placate the deities of the crops or the rain or the harvest.

Carl Lumholtz says [5] of the Tarahumare Indians in northwestern Mexico that they have six kinds of dances, all very ceremonial and of great antiquity, and that men and women never dance together as in our round dances. He found that the natives always had a flat, well-trodden open space in front of their cabins or huts, for the performance of these rites.

Further south in Mexico, Robert Redfield [6] tells about the tirelessness of the men of Tepoztlan, whose motion is rather one of leaping than dancing. In other places, also, the so-called dancing is often really a matter of leaping, and those who have seen the Indians of North America dance will recognize the resemblance. The reason for this is that the dancing usually takes place out of doors, so that uneven surfaces would interfere with gliding steps.

The writer I. M. Altamirano, who made a special study of the town of Tixtla in southern Mexico, says that in 1884 during certain Catholic festivals, special Aztec dances were performed. The participants were dressed in Aztec costume with headdresses and masks. They danced to the accompaniment of an Aztec drum which besides being a handsome specimen, looked as if it were a very old one. Meanwhile they sang or intoned a kind of chant with raucous

[5] Unknown Mexico, 336, 338-9. See also for melodies.
[6] Tepozlan, A Mexican Village.

words, that had all the earmarks of being pre-Spanish. The rest of
the Indians watched the dance with a respect which they made no
effort to dissimulate, meanwhile admiring the skill of the dancers.
As late as 1910, the writer has seen ceremonies within and in front
of country churches in Mexico, very similar to what these other
writers describe, in the south in the region of Mitla, and also in
villages much nearer to Mexico City.

In the spring of 1930 there was a festival at Taxco, in Mexico,[7]
in which five different dances followed one another, one of Moors,
one of little girls as shepherdesses, one called a Tiger dance (quite
pre-Spanish in its feeling), and finally two called the Three Powers.

There is more or less similarity between the celebrations belonging to definite seasons of the year, whether religious or secular,
and among the tribes who have had at least a little contact with the
whites, as we have seen, many of them show an interesting mixture of
Catholicism and nature-worship or superstition. Of these celebrations
Carnival and Corpus Christi are notable. There are accounts of
strange dances performed before the Host in the mountain churches
of Peru. In Bolivia, the national anthem is followed by a ritual song
for the crops, thus mixing modern nationalism with primitive nature
worship. In many cases Indian words are used instead of Spanish.
Animal masks are still worn (see illustration of a Yaqui dancer from
Mexico), in many of the out-of-the-way parts of the country, both
in Middle and South America. As long ago as 1614, in Lima, the
Church decreed that Deer head masks were a part of the idolatrous
belongings of the Indians and were to be summarily burned. At
other times as well, the Church has tried to prevent such manifes-
tations, but so far the hold has been too strong. Whatever the surface explanation may be for such forms of expression, the fact remains that there is a long unbroken tradition back of such symbolism, and that it is still a living tradition.

The rituals for the dead are characteristic in their way, and include mournful dances and songs. In the region of the northern
Andes, the wail is described as especially veiled and melancholy,
sometimes harsh and sometimes sweet. The women sing slowly,
without words, the men assisting; and they move in single file
around the corpse with their arms bent so that their hands are

---

[7] Described by Frances Toor in the magazine called **Mexican Folkways.**

DANCERS WITH FEATHER
HEAD DRESSES

DANCERS REPRESENTING
OLD MEN

TWO DRUMMERS WITH
SILVER BREASTPLATES

TWO DEVILS

Courtesy of Dr. Robert Hegner, Johns Hopkins University

YAQUI DANCER WITH DEER HEAD, MEXICO
Photographs by courtesy of Miss Frances Toor of
Mexico City

raised to the level of their shoulders with the palms turned down. This goes on outside the hut and lasts for half a day. Once in a while they pause for a breath or a drink.[8] Music for the funerals of little children is gay in contrast to the dirges for the grown ups, and consists of marches and songs, and the feeling is fairly general that the little child has been spared many hardships and is fortunate to be gathered among the angels so quickly.

All over the continent the villages have their own tutelary saints, and the saint's day gives a glorious opportunity for a celebration, usually combining religious and secular elements. There are processions and dances with costumes and decorations according to the ancient splendors of the tribe, wherever it may be, north or south.[9] Many times the village fair is included in the combination. We find similar accounts from the Andes and the east coast. From the northwest corner of the Argentine we hear of a festival, the preparations for which went on for days beforehand, involving a great deal of work over food and drink, not to mention costumes and decorations. Two villages or two sections of one village each chose their *comadre,* or directress of ceremonies. One of these goes to visit the other dressed in her very best, and surrounded by lads and maidens in all their finery. The next day the visit is returned in kind. The *comadre* must be dressed like an idol or an altar image, weighed down with ornaments, necklaces, rings and the like, mostly borrowed from the neighbors, who hope for return of favors on some future occasion. All colors, whether of dress or hangings, are the gaudiest possible, likewise the neckerchiefs of the boys and the trappings of the horses. The procession starts for the house of the other *comadre,* beginning slowly and solemnly, but breaking into ever-increasing speed, till they land at their destination on the dead run. The Indian orchestra, consisting of a sour clarinet, a cane flute, drums and a harp, (often the harpist is blind), begins to play frantically. When they all get together, come songs, dances, stories, and a general scramble for food and drink. It goes without saying that such festivities grow extremely riotous, but we are told that the Indians are so susceptible to the music of their native flutes, that the sound of one

---

[8] See Paul Marcoy, **A Journey across South America**. London, 1873.
[9] See article by R. J. Payro in the magazine **Musica de America**, Buenos Aires, March, 1921.

of these will still the tumult and set the people to listening. Sometimes they will be moved even to tears. The skeptically-minded might suggest alcohol as a contributing influence at this point, but the fact remains, nevertheless, that they do respond very readily to their music. Such gatherings as we have just described are the occasion for a real exchange of songs and ballads.

Again, from another district comes the account of a festival for which the chief sends word to all his tribe to meet in a certain picturesque valley. When they gather, the warriors make a large circle and each man drives his spear into the ground before him and kneels to it. Two young mares are driven up, one black to symbolize night, the other white to symbolize day, and each carrying a standard. Behind the kneeling men are a row of maidens dressed in black cloaks with ornaments on hair and neck. At the back the older Indians are grouped, also the musicians and trumpeters who give directions. The maidens dance to the sound of drums and flutes, and the mares race round the circle of warriors and maidens as a symbol of the sun's presence. At the end the Indians sing a monotonous chant.[10] At Copacabana, in Bolivia, there is a widely famed statue of the Virgin, to whose shrine pilgrimage is made yearly, from far and wide. This gives opportunity for dance and for songs and alas, for drinking as well.

Marcoy gives a vivid account of a fair as he found it in the Andes.[11]

"During the fifteen days that this fair lasts, the echoes of the *Puna,* accustomed to repeat only the lowing of herds and the sighs of the wind, resound with the rolling of drums, the tooting of tin trumpets, the hollow roaring of *pututus* (horns of Ammon), the melodious notes of the *queyna* and of the *pincullu* (two kinds of flutes or flageolets), and the strumming of the *charango,* the national

---

[10] See R. Rojas. La Literatura Argentina. 1917.
[11] Paul Marcoy, A Journey Across South America, Vol. 1.

three-stringed guitar, made by the Indians themselves with the half of a calabash, to which they attach a handle, and string it with cat-gut. The roaring of the crowd, the barking of dogs, the neighing of horses and mules, the hissing of frying-pans, and the crackling of fires kindled in the open air, form the bass of the wild concert. The amount of beef, mutton, llama's flesh, chickens, and guinea-pigs, devoured during the fifteen days of the fair, would serve to pro-vision a German duchy for a year. As for the quantity of brandy consumed, it is not possible to be exact, but we shall not be far wrong in believing that it would suffice to supply three rations a day to the crew of a fleet during its circumnavigation of the globe."

Squier tells about the *chuno* or potato festival of the Aymará Indians in the Andes mountains. "Each group danced vigorously to its united music, which were made up in volume what it lacked in melody—wild and piercing, yet lugubrious: the shrill pipe (pan-pipe) and the dull drum, with frequent blasts on cow's horns by amateurs among the spectators, filled the ear with discordant sounds. Every man seemed anxious to excell his neighbor in the energy of his movements, but the motions of the women were slow and steady. The music had its cadences, and the emphatic parts were marked by corresponding emphatic movements in the dance."

Dr. William M. McGovern [12] says that the Indians living in the northwest Amazon Basin near the boundary between Brazil and Columbia sang melodiously and in good accord. Some of the songs had words so old that the meaning of many words was lost, but the general understanding was there.

These Indians used flutes, drums, and for special ceremonies, trumpets which the women are never allowed to see on pain of death. They were real trumpets and each had a special secret name, which might never be spoken publicly. Each represented, and was supposed to embody, a special spirit of the jungle possessed of pe-culiar powers. He says that to the Indians these strange trumpets were no mere dead instruments of sounds, but the jungle spirits themselves, and that playing them brought communion with the ghostly beings.

Various travellers describe the interesting use of flutes in giving information or carrying on a conversation at a distance, across a

[12] **Jungle Paths and Inca Ruins.**

river, for instance, or from hill to hill. Among other primitive races drums are used in the same manner, and by varying the rhythm, the drummer can express himself in quite complicated ways.

Another description which comes from the depths of the Amazon jungle is as follows: [13] "Before the canoes were launched, a man fastened two upright forked sticks (on to the gunwale). On each side near the middle, about three and a half feet astern of one of these a cross-piece was laid on the bottom of the craft. To this were attached two shorter forked sticks. Between each pair of upright forked sticks was placed another cross piece, thus forming two horizontal bars parallel to each other, one only a few inches from the bottom of the boat and the other about a foot and a half above the gunwales. Next, four slabs of Caripari wood of varying thickness, about three feet long and eight inches wide, were suspended from these horizontal bars, so as to hang lengthwise of the canoe and at an angle of forty-five degrees. Each pair of slabs was perforated by a longitudinal slit and they were joined firmly at their extremities by finely carved and richly painted end pieces. The operator strikes the slabs with a wooden mallet or hammer, the head of which is wrapped with an inch of caoutchouc and then with a cover of thick tapir skin. Each section of the wooden slabs gives forth a different note when struck, a penetrating xylophonic tone, but devoid of the disagreeably metallic, disharmonic sounds of that instrument. The slabs of wood were suspended by means of thin fibre-cords, from the crosspieces, and in this manner all absorption by the adjacent material was done away with.

By means of many different combinations of the four notes obtained, which as far as I could ascertain, were Do-Re-Mi-La, the operator was enabled to send any message to a person who understood this code.—The four notes, given rapidly and repeated several times, represented the tuning up of the wireless calculated to catch the attention of the operator at the *maloca* or camp up creek— powerful sound—pleasant—musical echo—five rules.

Superstition plays an important role among the primitive tribes. The Tarahumares [14] are fond of music and use some of the Spanish types of instruments as well as their own, but they give the guitar the reputation of being the devil's choice for his own playing rather

---

[13] In the Amazon Jungle—Algot Lange.

than the violin; for in playing the latter the bow makes the shape of a cross against the strings. In Mexico, the Indians sing a special little song to the young turkeys, to make them grow well.

The Indians everywhere make music to lighten their toil, as do most primitive people. Marcoy speaks of the whistling of his pilot or headman to encourage the oarsmen. When they tired of the whistling they struck up a chorus that must have had some points in

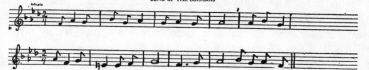

common with the familiar rounds of our youth. These men, when they are at work, have their hands occupied, so singing is the most obvious way of making music, but for the men who guide the llama caravans through the Andes, happiness and contentment seem to lie in having their little *quena* or flute, or a tiny guitar about two *hands* long. From our point of view both are ill-tuned and primitive, but they bring comfort to the Indian soul, so alone, and so tiny seeming, among those vast mountains.

Further to the east, in central Brazil, live the Bororo tribe of Indians. They are primarily singers rather than instrumentalists, according to Henry Savage Landor. They recognize three types of rhythm, one not unlike a slow waltz, plaintive and melancholy; the second warlike, loud and vivacious; and the third, sad. As concise a statement as this is not often found, with such definite detail, and whether it is due to the especial musical gifts of the Bororos or to the patient and pains-taking efforts of the writer, would be hard to say. Landor next states that the songs of this tribe group themselves as hunting-songs, war-songs, love-songs and descriptive songs or recitations. Their voices are soft and musical even in conversation, and he tells us that they are fond of improvising, so that no song was

[14] See Lumholtz, Idem.

ever twice alike; also that they liked singing in chorus or an alternation of solo and chorus. From other sources one finds that these people are adepts in cross-rhythms, the voices taking one quite complicated rhythm while the percussion instruments, clappers and rattles, take another.

The foregoing statement about the Bororos shows at a glance the types of songs to be found among most primitive groups, songs of war, the hunt, love, and ballads or something analogous. In the latter the subjects are often accounts of local annals and heroes and in that way take the place of written history. Thus the groups of songs may in reality be considered as songs of communal or personal life. In this way, the topic of a song is sometimes local and sometimes general. The emotional and technical characteristics of music are either of local or general significance. To those habituated to Indian music these earmarks are recognizable. Thus, Ricardo Rojas tells us that the *Guarany* Indians have distinct elements that separate their music from the *Araucanian* or again from the *Quechua*. This may sometimes be a question of melodic cadences, but often it is a matter of rhythm-patterns. For the same thing would apply in South America which the specialists have found to be true of North America. That is, among the tribes on the northern continent, scholars like Mary Austin have found that the musical rhythms of the different tribes are patterned oftentimes on the rhythms of their habitual occupations. A tribe whose life is spent largely in canoes or on horseback would be apt to sing in the accentuation that is the daily accompaniment of their lives. The tribes which have a craft of one kind or another that tends to rhythmic motion, pottery making or weaving for example, are apt to have their musical thoughts run in these grooves. Farming has various rhythmic actions and those patterns would easily present themselves as the background for song rhythm.

As more and more contacts are made between the backward tribes and the civilized cities, the older forms of song tend to die out, or at least to be relegated to the children, with a sense of grown-up scorn underlying their use. Still later comes a time when the city-minded group, educators or antiquarians, take up what remains of the old songs or customs, and teach them in the schools or for festivals and in that way preserve them, but turn them into a

FIESTA IN QUILIAPAN, MEXICO
Photographed by Miss Yoch and Miss Council

FESTIVAL IN MEXICO

Photograph by courtesy of Hugo Brehme, Mexico City

sophisticated thing that has lost its spontaneity. At least this phase preserves valuable material, but the childhood of the race has passed in making the change. So now the children are being definitely trained in the ancient traditional dances, to be performed on festival occasions. Hopefully at the same time they are being given an interest and a sympathy in the traditions of their forebears so that they will be able to assist in the future in working toward the right attitude about their racial inheritance and its preservation. For the Latin-Americans possess a heritage of inestimable value to bring to the study of the development of the human race, and moreover, the opportunity of "catching it alive", a contribution that is denied to most of the rest of the world.

Chapter Four

INSTRUMENTS AND SONGS

AN old Spanish proverb says, *"Decidnos las canciones de un pueblo y os diremos sus leyes, sus costumbres y su historia."* Or in English, "Tell us the songs of a people, and we will tell you its laws, its customs and its history." So we come back to the same point that we have stressed at intervals in this book, that the folk music, and even the sophisticated music of a given people grow out of its' life and reflect it.

The foregoing chapters are mainly devoted to descriptions of the instruments and scales of Latin American music, or the times and seasons for it's performance, or the emotions it is expected to enhance. Now we shall glance at some of the characteristic songs and dances, of the different regions. Many of the songs overlap into the dance class or vice versa, for instance, a dance like the *Habanera* might be doubly listed, for the tunes that are used for dancing are not used for the sung Habanera.[1] Also, many of the songs and dances overlap political boundaries, but in that case the performance has local qualities; so that the Argentine *cueca* does not interest the Chilean performer or vice-versa. And the Uruguayan Maxixe does not count for the Brazilian or the reverse.

The accompanying chart cannot hope to include every name of song and dance, but it does give all the more familiar kinds. Many are found in more than one country, as we have just said, so that an arbitrary classification by political boundaries is not really fair. For song forms flow freely wherever the mood of the song finds a sympathetic channel. Thus the sad melodies wrung from the soul of the mountain singer by the stern conditions of his world, take on a different profile when they reach the fertile plains, and the men of the Pampas do not sing the mournful *Yaraví* of Peru.

---

[1] The Habanera rhythm is familiar to many Anglo-Saxons.

During colonial times what might be considered a normal amount of evolution in music was artifically slowed down by the fact that Spain restricted the commercial and cultural contacts of the colonies by forbidding all trade with other countries and limiting the number of her own fleets during the year. The result of such prohibitions, from the musical standpoint, was that the colonies clung to archaic types of instrument or song, long after Spain herself had evolved new kinds. Thus, the *bihuela,* a more ancient predecessor of the guitar, was still familiar in Spanish America when the mother country had discarded it for the newer instrument. Other old-fashioned instruments also held their own in the western hemisphere longer than in Europe. The fact that the Indian is a naturally conservative creature added to this tendency. So, the full-blooded Indian of the present day still uses some of the pre-Spanish drums, flutes, trumpets and so on, the names varying according to geographic location. The guitar family has become thoroughly acclimated and is found in a variety of forms. It varies according to district, in size, number of strings and name, for example, *tiple, charango, guitarrita, cuatro, seis, doce,* etc. Among the people of mixed blood one finds sundry members of the violin, harp and wood-wind tribe; while the sophisticated musicians employ all the instruments available for the complete modern orchestra. The aforementioned instruments might be said to be ubiquitous, but there are others that are known and loved in certain more or less restricted areas, without being at home elsewhere. For instance, in the Andes, a type of primitive little flute called *Quena* is the almost constant companion of the llama drivers, and others who are porters or burden bearers, and who seem to derive cheer from its uncouth sounds. The panpipes or syrinx which they use is called *Zampoña* and is made of many sizes and of different substances. Again, in Cuba, Venezuela and also further south, there is a kind of gourd rattle called *Maraca,* which is used in dancing. Originally employed only for religious ceremonies, it is now used for secular music as well. It is found at times as far away as Columbia and Ecuador. In Central America one finds the *Marimba,* an instrument not unlike the Xylophone in character, but greatly enlarged. It has graded sizes of gourds or wooden boxes for resonators. The frame on which they are hung is often as much as five or six feet long, and three or four players are needed to play

ALL SAINTS DAY AT MOROCOCHA, PERU
Harps, panpipes, double flutes
Photographs by courtesy of M. Guy Edwards

INDIAN DANCE, JULY, 1927. ANDES PLATEAU, BOLIVIA
The bull is made of the hide of a yearling. The toreador's ornaments
are real silver. Photographs by courtesy of A. F. Bennett

one instrument.[2] The illustration on page 62 shows a type of harp that is found throughout the central region of the Andes, quite obviously home-made and curiously different from what the harp is among us.

With such a category of instruments, the modal range would naturally vary from the few notes of the little *Quena,* or mountain flute, through numerous other instruments of increasing range, to those that have the full possibilities of scale like the string family. The five tone scale as used in modern Indian music,[3] makes for somberness and melancholy, and has a tendency toward a descending melodic line. This gives a flavor quite apart from European tunes of the same scope. Any one familiar with the music of the North American Indians will recognize the same type in their songs. Among the Negro population in Brazil one finds often a six tone scale, lacking the leading tone. For the origin of this scale one should hark back to Africa. Certain intervals are much used in Latin America, the seventh, the fourth, and the third. In the northern Andes, the third often shows an alternation between major and minor, or is a kind of neutral, giving to any melody a haunting quality of real charm. Among all these races the use of the minor mode does not necessarily mean sadness and melancholy, but often passion. Alternation between major and minor within one melody are frequent, usually between related major and minor, but occasionally between tonic major and minor. There is apt to be a generous use of grace notes, often involving a skip of quite a large inter-between the ornament and the note. This gives an effect unlike what we are accustomed to hear.

As to rhythms, 2/4 is much used, as in the Habanera and the Tango, also 3/4, and the delightful, supple Spanish 3/8. 5/4 and 6/8 are familiar as well. Great freedom and imagination are shown in the use of these rhythms, as also in the use of two or more against each other, and in the variety of detail as compared to the folk music of other races. The Cubans excel in this rhythmic gift, often using five or six simultaneous rhythms. Many times one finds sudden

---

[2] The Marimba is also known in Africa. Compare the Hungarian instrument called **Cembalom.**

[3] See any of the writings of M. Béclard D'Harcourt, also D. A. Robles, and the **Cancionero Incaico** of V. G. Cáceres and V. Forte, for numerous examples.

changes of rhythms, or alternations between two and three part rhythms, as for instance, two two beat measures followed by one of three, giving a unit of seven. The custom of playing an accompaniment that has well-accented first beats, while the melody runs in decapitated phrases starting on the last half of the weak beat following, gives an emotional intensity which is most appropriate to certain kinds of songs. It is especially found in the Habanera or Danza. Post war jazz, with its stress on African rhythms, has temporarily influenced much of the music of Latin America, but it is to be hoped that this influence will not be permanent.

From the point of view of harmony, the possibilities are only lately being recognized, as for a long time even quite good musicians were satisfied to use a monotonous repetition in their chord successions. As a rule, melody and rhythm have interested Latin-American composers more than harmony and counterpoint, this, even among the quite sophisticated ones.

In regard to the songs and dances themselves, we find that these also have a threefold source, Spanish, Indian and mixed. In Brazil, Venezuela and Cuba and the other islands the negro element is added. Those with Spanish names, *Fandango, Folía, Zarabanda, Seguidilla* have often suffered some kind of a sea change in their transfer to the new country, but the underlying type is usually discernible. Mexico, for instance, has many delightful examples called *Malagueña,* but to one familiar with the Gypsy *Malagueña* of southern Spain, it is quite obvious that this *Malagueña* has attributes not found in the Spanish dance.

The largest number of songs and dances is to be included in the *Mestizo* group. It is apt to be broad and symmetrical in form with a charm and grace that are absent from the Indian type. It differs from the Spanish songs of the *Malagueña* and *Rondeña* class, with their freedom of movement. The native of the western hemisphere is a fine improviser when it suits his mood, and uses his gift with skill and grace. His gift is more likely to show itself in suddenly inspired verses of some definite pattern, than in the overlaying of spontaneous ornament around the melody. This latter is what the Spanish gypsy revels in doing.

The age of a folk-song is hard to determine at any time, except from internal evidence, structure, style, and the general atmosphere, and the written versions often vary so much from those sung, as to be considered almost as different compositions at times. But of the Mexican songs, Manuel M. Ponce says that they are for the most part of comparatively recent origin, perhaps the latter half of the eighteenth century. He cites one document in confirmation—a proclamation of the year 1802-3. The Viceroy then in office, Don Felix Berenguer de Marquina, forbade "the pernicious and improper dance named *Jarabe gatuno*" (that is catlike), and he went on to enumerate what he considered its many bad qualities.

The words of the songs cover a wide range of subjects and feelings, not to mention varieties of poetic technique. Both folk singers and sophisticated poets enjoy complicated rhythm patterns and manage them cleverly. Often they are satisfied with assonance where we in our use of English would feel the need of real rhyme, but with the flowing cadences of Spanish, assonance is all that is needed. Everybody, whether of the sophisticated or the unsophisticated class, enjoys verses or couplets that have what the Spaniards call *Sal,* or salt. Our nearest translation is perhaps tang, or verve, or spice, but no one of these represents all that a Spaniard or Spanish American thinks of when he uses the word. So when plenty of *Sal* is present in a verse, composer, singer and audience all enjoy themselves keenly. Such verses often take on the attributes of a proverb. The use of metaphor or simile about nature is almost universal, and shows a real love for it. Birds, flowers, trees, are all used with poetic and sympathetic touch.

There are several ways in which songs and dances may be classified; that is, by their origins, whether imported, mixed, or native; or by their functions, whether religious or secular, ceremonial or personal. Religious songs, such as the *Alabado* are universal. Maudslay gives an unforgettable description of another such style of song, the *Alborada*.[4] The secular music includes of course, danceable music and songs. Perhaps the most interesting classification from the point of view of folk-lore is according to whether the songs and dances involve public ceremonials, or whether they originate from individual

---

[4] The sound of a boy's shrill voice chanting a few bars of melody, which was caught up by a chorus of men's voices a fifth lower, and repeated again and again as the sound rapidly approached our tent, and then died away in the distance. It was the morning hymn of a company of Indian pilgrims returning from the shrine of the Black Christ at Esquipulas. Later—they chanted the quaint hymn at night before the shrine.

or personal emotions. Ceremonial music has to do with crops, har-
vests, labor of various kinds, and with public expressions of joy or
mourning. The personal group includes songs of love, personal sorrow or joy, and most of the children's group, as well as songs of the
ballad type. The latter are known as *Corridos,* and are practically
universal throughout Latin America. They are the logical descendants of the early Spanish ballads, and during the entire pioneer
period were a god-send to the people during long evenings around
the fire, when there were almost no books, no electric lights, and
little outside news. But there was always a chance to sing, far better
than most people get nowadays.

The subjects of *Corridos* may be political or amorous or humorous, but must primarily be such as would interest the peasant or
middle-class person, and must have news value. The stories they tell
either idolize the hero or turn him into a kind of demon. Madero
was much beloved by the makers of *Corridos,* Carranza not so. Within two days after the death of Pancho Villa, the street singers were
shouting endless verses about him. Unless a song of this kind has
some sort of permanent appeal in either words or music, it tends to
die out in time, as new heroes rise out of the level of mediocrity.
Corridos are created by folk musicians blessed with a gift for improvising and are sometimes very primitive in form and prosody.
The man who starts the song improvises, and many of those who
sing it later, add verses or modify words or music. Thus, it will be
seen that improvisation, a gift that has almost died out among the
more sophisticated nations, is still a living talent among these people.
The current versions of such ballads are really the result of community creation, and belong in the class of real folk-music. If a song
of this character grows popular enough, it may be printed on sheets
of cheap paper like the old English *Broadsides,* and spread abroad by
the thousand. Moreover, many people in the country keep copybooks
full of their favorites. As a rule, the idea of interpretation seems to be
to shout them at the top of lusty lungs.

Corridos, are, as we have said, well nigh ubiquitous, but there
are many types of song and dance that belong to a restricted area
only. Thus in Mexico, for instance, the *Jarabe* is considered more
than any other, as the national dance, and is especially beloved in the
state of Jalisco. It is said to have originated among the Andalusian

gypsies around Cadiz, and it is described by a Mexican writer, as *"baile tan bullicioso y nacional"*, that is, exceedingly lively or boisterous and national. It is a graceful, spirited dance of one man and one woman, and gives a real opportunity for good technique. It is usually written in 6/8 time, though sometimes in 3/4 or 2/4. Occasionally, there will be two measures of three beats each, followed by one of two, so that the melodic phrase is irregular, with an eight beat unit. The melodic line is simple and simply harmonized, and as a rule the song has piquancy and charm. The *Jarabe Tapatío* is a great favorite, the *Jarabe Gatuno*, as previously mentioned, has made a bad name for itself. Other dances familiar in Mexico are the *Habanera, Folía, Fandango,* and for songs, there are many, *Mañanitas,* (morning songs), *Sones, Charaperas,* sung when under the influence

LAS MAÑANITAS

of *Charapa,* a local alcoholic beverage, and so on.

From South America the names most familiar to us are the *Tango* and the *Maxixe.* The former is familiar in Argentina, Brazil, and Uruguay. Its' origin is ascribed in various ways, but is often explained as Andalusian. The Brazilian Tango is further removed in any case from the Andalusian, and is more vivid than the Argentine. It is familiar enough to North Americans not to need a detailed description, but it seems to be the general opinion that it is more gracefully and agreeably danced in the country districts than among the lower classes in the cities. The basis of the accompaniment is not unlike that of the *Habanera,* but it often lacks the variety of detail and interest of the latter. The *Tango* has also reached Mexico, and in all these countries the detail varies, so that the Uruguayan dances it according to *his* taste, and the Mexican to his, etc. The *Batuque* and the *Samba* or *Zamba* (according to one's geographical location) are also characteristic, and imply an infusion of African elements, when the word has the Brazilian spelling with an S. Among the ignorant negroes there is still more or less belief in witchcraft, and as the corresponding negro, in the Carribean Islands has his *Vodoo* with its rites, so the Brazilian negro has his *Macumbu* with its' ritual. This often includes music, but it is almost impossible for the white person to hear it. The *Modinha* is a song found in

Brazil, to which it was brought from the Mother Country, Portugal, where it developed out of the early Portuguest form, *Serranilla.* The diminutive "inha" is added to the word "moda", mood or style, and this implies a fragment in a certain mood, or a little song in a given mood. *Rondas, Toadas, Cocos, Fandango*s, are all familiar names too, as well as certain *polcas* and *mazurcas* which show in their names one of the results of the influx of settlers from Slavic countries during the last half century or so.

The Argentine Republic is the habitat of a numerous family of songs and dances that have their roots in the life of the Pampas. The *Vidala* and the *Vidalita,* or little *Vidala,* grew up among the Gauchos,

though some authorities would trace them to more remote origins, and they spread over into Bolivia and Peru. They are more popular in Northern Argentina than Southern. The name, in any case, means life, coming from the Spanish word, "vida". That is, the song is a little fragment out of Life. Each *Vidalita* is made up of endless verses, and one characteristic of the type is that the word *Vidalita* itself is repeated after the first and third line of every stanza. The rhythm of the Vidalita is usually either 2/4 or 4/4, and of the *Vidala* a three part beat. Joaquin V. Gonzalez says that the *Vidalita* belongs especially to the season of the year when the yellow fruit of the algarrobo tree is ripening, for then the people on the ranches get out their guitars and drums, and the girls their gayest costumes and ornaments, and every one makes merry.

The Pericon is perhaps the most popular dance of the Argentine, and is danced by a number of couples who stand in a double row, facing each other, alternating men and girls. The first few moments of the music are given over to preening themselves, smoothing skirts, settling hats, and so on. Then they go forward and back, and left and right in contrary motion, eight times. Each man lifts one hand over his head, and takes the girl's lifted hand, the other hand around the girl's waist. Next, each man goes to the girl in front and executes a quick turn with hands raised or extended, then back to his partner. The men kneel on the left knee and each girl waltzes around her partner. The girls place a hand on the partner's shoulder, palm up; The man takes it gently and makes a circle around his girl and goes back to position. The girls take hands and slowly complete a circle. The men make a circle outside in the opposite direction and back to position. Next they do a right and left, then the men bow to their partners and flourish their hats gracefully. The director or as he is called, the *Bastonero* shouts *Viva el Pericon*. Everybody returns to position and shouts *Viva* in conclusion.

The *Triste* is closely related to the *Vidalita* and is generally supposed to have its real home in Peru, and to have spread over to the Argentine, especially the northern part. There are certain local differences. The stanzas of the *Triste* are decimas and not four line stanzas, as are those of the Vidalita. The *Cielito* started as a type of love-song, but grew into a political song during the years of fighting for freedom. Its regular pattern is a three-part rhythm, with a melody based on two bars of tonic and two of dominant chords in the accompaniment. The *Ranchero* is rather a late comer, and is a development from the polka. The *Chacarera* is danced by four dancers and involves some delightfully vigorous and spirited foot work.

In Chile, perhaps the most familiar name outside the boundaries of the country itself, is the *Cueca or Zamacueca,* a dance in 3/8 time. It was popular to a high degree, through the colonial period, and more so in the country than in the city. Within the last generation society has abandoned the *Cueca* for other more cosmopolitan dances, leaving it to the lower classes, with whom it amounts almost to a passion.

To find a description of the Chilean *Cueca* as it was danced in the first quarter of the nineteenth century, we can not do better than to go back to Captain Hall, whom we quoted several times in the course of Chapter 2. He says that, "One of their favorite figures begins in a manner not unlike our minuet, with slow and apparently unpremeditated movements; the parties approaching and receding from each other, occasionally joining hands, swinging round, and sometimes stooping so as to pass under each other's arms. These figures admit the display of much grace and ease, and inevitably betray any awkwardness of manner. The slow movements last a minute or two, after which the measure suddenly changes from a dull monotonous tune to a quick and varied air, loudly accompanied by the drum and all the voices. At this instant the dancers commence a sort of shuffling step, during which the feet do not slide, but rather stamp with great rapidity on the ground. At the moment of this change in time, the dancers dart forward toward each other waving their handkerchiefs affectedly before them. They do not actually meet, but, when almost touching, pass and continue around each other in circles larger or smaller, according to the space allowed; accompanying these rotatory motions by various gesticulations, especially that of waving their handkerchiefs over their partner's heads. There was a striking difference between the manner in which these dances were performed by the town's people, and by the Guassos or countrymen; the latter having always the advantage both in skill and elegance." In this and various other dances, there is much snapping of the fingers, *never* castanets, and many of them include graceful waving of handkerchiefs, and occasionally also, flourishes with a hat. The *Cueca* resembles in type the Spanish *Jota* or the *Fandango.* The latter is also danced in Peru where it is more lyric and closer to the Spanish than it is in Bolivia. In Peru, Bolivia and Ecuador, the most widespread of all the songs are the *Yaraví* and the *Triste*. The word *Yaraví* is a Spanish version of the Quechua word, *Haravi* meaning lament. The German writer, Albert Friedenthal, traces the word *Yaraví* back to an Arabic origin, through the Spaniards. He points out that the often-used Arabic exclamation "Ya Rabi", (Oh Lord!) is a lamenting phrase, which must have been familiar to many of the early Spaniards. Analogies are dangerous, but there are many elements of Arabic culture that found their way to the Andes during colonial times. *Yaraví* has a meaning therefore, similar to that of the

HARAHUI OR YARAVÍ FROM CUZCO

Spanish word *Triste,* sad or sorrowful; Both songs are sung as their names would imply, with poignant feeling, often with languor and a certain nobility.[5] The time signature for both is generally 6/8, but may vary. The *Yaraví* is recited or sung by one or more voices, and for subject matter usually has some element of unfortunate love or of sorrow for the dead. The *Marinera* is another familiar and similar song of this region.

The songs of Cuba and the other Carribean Islands have qualities all their own, in melody, rhythm and instruments. Of the instruments, some belong to the melodic group, including some strange clay things of the flute family. Guitars of course, may be heard everywhere, and percussion instruments include rasping-sticks, gourd resonators, and many kinds of drums. The Cubans gift for mixed rhythms amounts almost to genius, five or six different ones often being played simultaneously by one small group of performers. The three varieties of songs most often heard are the *Son,* the *Merengue* and the *Habanera*. The last of these is well known to those of us who live in the Anglo-Saxon countries. But of all, the *Son* is the most varied and interesting. It is usually performed by a group of five or six Negro players, any one of whom may burst into song at any moment in addition to carrying on his instrumental performance.

---

[5] See M. Béclard D'Harcourt **Melodies Populaires Indiennes.** Introductory Essay.

One writer describes the typical dance orchestra of Cuba as consisting of a clarinet, two flutes, cornet, two trombones, or bassoons, bombardino, kettle drum, two marugas (rattles), güiro (rasping stick), guitar and a harp, if possible.

This part of the subject would not be complete without touching on one picturesque custom which has been universal in the past throughout Latin America. As life grows more stereotyped, it is alas! dying out. This is colloquially known as "Playing the Bear", *Haciendo el oso,* and without this custom, courting could not have been carried on all these years. Many descriptions have been written about it:—the swain and the maiden murmuring sweet nothings to each other through the iron grille of her window. This was permissible during many hours of daytime or evening, and was the only way in which they could grow acquainted. For strict conventions made an almost orientally circumscribed life for girls, and prevented a young couple from meeting without being heavily chaperoned by their elders. This was the case until almost the wedding day. So it

MEJORANA FROM PANAMA

goes without saying that there are endless charming songs for expressing love, and that they run the whole gamut of the emotions, joyous, sad, doubtful, languishing, playful, triumphant.

In all the various countries, national songs are to be found, the product of the period when the spirit of independence was developing. This desire first showed itself in the course of the seventeenth century, and culminated in the series of revolutions that dotted the first half of the nineteenth century with courage and suffering and bloodshed. During that time all the colonies broke away from the mother country and set up their own governments. The actual dates varied in each case, but those do not concern us. From the musical standpoint, the interest lies in the crop of hymns, songs and ballads that grew up everywhere. Such compositions, written as they are for a special purpose, *not* primarily musical, do not make as satisfying music as those created for sheer beauty and emotion. But as the expression of the spirit of their time, they are worthy of attention. There are many ballads or *corridos* telling the exploits of the national heroes and heroines of the conflicts, for there were heroines as well as heroes, as is attested by the ballad of the beautiful Policarpa Salabarrieta. She was a Colombian revolutionist, who after many activities was executed at the same time with a group of men, and she spent her last moments exhorting them to courage. This is only one of many such ballads, which for the unlettered folk go to make up the record of their history and ideals, their dreams and the effort at realization.

Two songs of this general character are *La Golondrina* and *La Paloma,* both from Mexico, but they call for little special comment. It appears that the words of the former are a translation from the French by Francisco Martinez de la Rosa. About La Paloma, perhaps the most interesting information is that it was a favorite song of the unfortunate Empress Carlota. The music was written by the composer Yradier. These two songs are perhaps the best known of any Spanish American compositions, but there are many others just as worthwhile and as characteristic and with much more originality.

During the middle of the nineteenth century, Europe as well as the western hemisphere was the scene of revolutions. Curious echoes of those troubled times in Europe sometimes found their last vibrations in the new world, for in many cases the revolutionists if

defeated, were exiled and fled to one or the other of these western
continents. They came with high hopes of finding political freedom,
and brought with them the songs that had inspired them during
the conflict, whatever else they may have had to leave behind. One
such song, now called *El Trobador*,* is well known in Southern
California. In its present version it has a melody of unusual grace,
with words which really make it into a serenade. It is the man who
sings, and he describes himself as an exile suffering distress and
poverty. To jump from Southern California to Poland seems a far
cry, but persons familiar with the songs of that country have only
to compare the tune of El Trobador with that of the Polish revo-
lutionary song called *Valiant Lagienka,* to realize that the two songs
are really built on the same pattern. In the second section the curves
of melody follow each other, but with the difference that the California tune lies much of the time an interval of a third above the
Polish tune. This gives it greater emotional warmth, and so to say,
latinizes it. Additional corroboration of the probable journeys of
this song come with the discovery that groups of Poles settled in and
around Santa Barbara about the middle of the nineteenth century.
Probably when they sang their beloved songs, the Spanish Califor-
nians heard and liked this tune; so they added the upper voice, a
third above the original, for duets in thirds are a passion with all
the race. The next step would be the words, and here the idea of the
exile in his poverty makes a plausible sounding link. Undoubtedly
many such transformations must have occurred, but one cannot often
retrace as many links in the connection as in this case.

Both in the words and music of their songs, Latin American performers have an almost unfailing sense of artistic values which saves
them from going to extremes. They have a real gift in balancing
sections in their relationship to one another. From an Anglo-Saxon
point of view, the sentiment is sometimes too heavily laid on, but
that is a question of taste, and they in turn think we are too re-
pressed in expression.

A characteristic picture of native musicians, which might fit
almost anywhere in Spanish America, is the following;—The vio-
linist, in working clothes, first plays the theme, then the harpist

* See "Folk Songs from Mexico and South America", Eleanor Hague.
Pub. H. W. Gray, New York.

repeats it in the form of chords for the right hand, accompanied by a syncopated bass for the left hand. The guitarist strikes sweeping chords, (rasgueando) in a separate rhythm. Drums and other percussion instruments enter by degrees and the whole makes a little orchestra with individuality, fervor and charm all its' own.

Chapter Five

THE SOPHISTICATED MUSIC OF THE
PRESENT AND ITS' PROSPECTS

URING the colonial period of Latin-America, there were only slight opportunities for cultural contacts with the rest of the world. In later times, as those contacts increased, they ran east and west rather than north and south, bringing together the Latin civilizations in the two hemispheres, and likewise the Anglo-Saxon. Thus, long after Europe had begun to know and understand Latin-America, we in North America remained woefully in the dark. The result is that present conditions come upon us as a real surprise. This period of isolation had however its very definite compensations. The people had a chance to develop along individual lines, and this, in spite of the temporary fashion for imitating Italian and French models referred to earlier. Moreover, the influence of the Catholic church tended strongly toward a conservatism which at times was intense. The significance of this statement and its far-reaching effects will be understood, when we realize that until the last half century, church music was practically the only model of sophisticated European music available for those who did not dwell in the coastal cities. The folk inland had their church music, the secular music whose tradition they had inherited, and the simple Mestizo or Indian, or in places, Negro, the songs and dances they heard around them. (See tunes with date of 1717, p. 37.) So it was natural enough that the beginnings of the educated music should have been slight, but even so there were a few notable figures among the cultured musicians. In Brazil one of the early ones was Carlos Gomez, born in the State of São Paulo in 1839. His father was an orchestral conductor and teacher of music, and gave the boy his early training. Later he went to Italy to study, where he came under the influence of Verdi and his contemporaries. Gomez wrote in both the larger and smaller forms, including operas, a symphonic poem called *Colombo,* and many songs and short numbers. Among his operas, the most famour is *"O Guarany"*, written on an Indian tale. It was much admired by Verdi when it was performed with great success at La Scala in Milan. In it he used a few Indian themes, but his treatment and technique were perfectly Italian. Nevertheless, he was of importance as being the pioneer in the use of native material. In Argentina, at approximately the same time, there were two musicians, one named Alcorta and the other Esnaola, who did much to build up the foundations of Argentine art, although they did not have as thorough a training as Gomez, and their fame did not spread beyond the borders of their own country. The names of the pioneers in the other countries are hard to gather, for records are few and slight.

Later, the great Venezuelan pianist, Teresa Carreño, gained a world wide reputation as a virtuoso, playing in all the big centers of the world, and with all the noteworthy orchestras. There were other musicians worthy of notice, but the limits of one small volume would be quickly over-stepped to mention all; the names given are of especial importance as leaders.

While this conscious art music was feeling its way forward, the characteristic songs and dances described in chapter four, continued to grow up from the reactions of the people to the life about them. At first many of the educated musicians scorned these simpler creations as belonging to the Indians or the lower classes; but the times have changed, and now the characteristic dances and songs are receiving the intelligent consideration they deserve from scholars.[1]

In Argentina, in Mexico, in Brazil, Chile and Peru such work is going on, and it is of the most careful and accurate nature. For a number of years there has been flourishing society in Buenos Aires, formed for the preservation, development, and diffusion of the native arts. They cultivate the charming old dances and songs, and take a pride in them that is not merely antiquarian, as the tradition is still a living influence.[2]

The sympathetic study of Inca music dates from approximately 1910 or 1912. It includes excellent field work by a number of devotees,

---

[1] A complete list of such scholars is impossible for new workers come into the field every little while, but a number of names will be found in the bibliography.

[2] As the result of this impetus, Argentina has a long list of published material to her credit.

and more recently also, good comparative studies. (See Bibliography) Mexico has also been active in this type of undertaking; and Mexico like Brazil is large enough to have tribes in the back country of very varied habits and cultures. Most of the smaller countries are beginning to awaken to the possibilities of the subject.

Many authors, in writing of their hopes and ambitions, believe that the road for the future lies in the fusion of native material with the later cosmopolitan developments in musical expression. The subject is a debatable one, and may be approached from various angles. On the negative, such an able and well-trained musician as Juan José Castro of Buenos Aires would argue that the expression of the human soul is more important than the racial elements. However, the other side argues well and what is more, has some excellent music to show for it, of which we shall speak in detail later. There are a number of clever exponents of the nationalist point of view, and the tenor of their arguments shows that race consciousness has become a real factor in their reasoning. Thus, the Argentine writer, Gaston O. Talamon says,[3] "All the related Ibero-Americans are fired with the same artistic flame, (yearning, passion, inquietude), and are working toward an Americanization in music based on the indigenous and mestizo song." (This, of course, means Americanization from a Latin-American standpoint, not North American). In Mexico Romero and others present approximately the same idea in different words. Musicians elsewhere talk about nationalism in music, and protest against the complete Germanization of the art. They insist that German music is not the only norm of musical beauty, and say quite justly that other countries have traditions of tonal art that go as far or further back and have just as much foundation[4]. The musicians of all the Latin-American countries are urged to be themselves. Such urging is naturally having its effect in educating public opinion, both in getting away from mere imitation, and in developing a respect for the value of their own disappearing folk material. For as we have said previously, modernization is taking place for good or for ill, in Ibero-America as elsewhere. The large cities have all the most modern attributes, and more and more, machinery is getting

---

[3] Un cuarto de siglo de musica Argentina.
[4] See the writings of J. B. Trend on Spanish music also H. G. Farmer on Arabic music, also The Music of Ancient Arabia and Spain, translated from the Spanish of J. Ribera by Eleanor Hague.

into the sugar factories, tractors on to the big ranches, and steam-
boats in ever increasing numbers on the rivers, and so on. All these
things go toward standardizing life, and stressing the city elements
rather than the country and tribal.

This is not utterly to be regretted however for many valuable
changes have come with the modernizing enthusiasm, and even the
radio and the phonograph are of real help in diffusing the characteristic music beyond the bounds of any one country. Many organizations like choral societies, philharmonic orchestras and smaller
groups have come into being. Mexico had its *Sociedad Filarmonica*
as early as 1839, and other countries can show comparable dates.
Some of these groups, like the orquestas tipicas, have travelled far
afield, and made fine reputations for themselves. Music festivals, large
and small, take place in Mexico, the Argentine, Cuba and elsewhere.
Conservatories have grown up in practically all the cities of any
size, with excellent training in musicianship. The result is a public
of exceptional intelligence and training, among whom are found occasional artists of rare merit. The younger generation makes a good
showing, with many men and women who are winning their laurels.
The Brazilian pianist, Guiomar Novaes is one of the best known;
another of her country women, also a pianist, is Ofelia Nacimiento;
José Mojica, the Mexican tenor is well known in the United States,
as is Margarita D'Alvarez, the Peruvian contralto; and there are
many more.

These are only four names out of many. And now, what of the
composers and the use they may make of all this wealth of material,
Indian, Mestizo and Spanish, and the inspiration it may engender?

The Spanish Composers have blazed the way, for men like
Granados, Albeñiz, Pedrell, Falla, Turina, and others have shown
to a skeptical world what can be done with national idiom enriched
by art. As for folk idiom, Latin-American people have all the resources of the Iberian peninsula and Latin-America as well, that
is, both hemispheres. For, as was indicated in chapter two, Iberian
tradition mounts into the dim antiquity of the Orient, through the
Arabs. As the colonists have come from all sections of the peninsula,
it follows that the different types of song found in the mother country are familiar friends when they come to this side of the Atlantic.
During the beginning of the colonial period, it was natural that

more settlers should have come from the maritime provinces than from inland, but as time went on, we find all the provinces represented. Thus there are local settlements made up mainly of Basques, others of Catalonians, others again of Andalusians, and so on. In each case these people have contributed at least the traditions of their regional songs and dances; often their instruments as well; thus, the very individual Basque rhythm, 5/8 as it is found in their dance, the *Zortzico*. The special style of the *Jota* as danced in Aragon or in Valencia, the oriental flavor of Andalusia and the Gypsy tradition are all in the blood of one or another of the immigrants. So it has come about that the various elements familiarly known as the Spanish musical idiom, and, though less well known, the Portuguese musical idiom, (similar to the Spanish but with certain definite variations), have all found a foothold in Ibero-America. The composer may therefore draw from these sources by right of sympathy and inheritance. The vast indigenous field lies open to the composer also, with its funds of melody and rhythm. The emotions of this music are intense and melancholy, and its melodic contours thoroughly individual. From both sides and from the fusion, the people have a love of ceremony that lends dignity to what they do, and the early life of the colonies was certainly conducive to the development of song.

During the last generation a start has been made in the direction of a more cosmopolitan angle of vision. To the invaluable basis of folk-music, the musicians are adding the latter day experience of musicians in other parts of the world. It is to be hoped that their own gifts of expression will be strong enough to mold the cosmopolitan influences to their needs, rather than to be swamped thereby. A real technical equipment is thus in process of development. The modernist movement in the arts has reached Mexico and all the South American countries to a greater or lesser degree, and music is in the forefront of the impetus. The musicians are writing in all the smaller forms and branching out into the larger. Among the pioneers in the movement is the Brazilian, Alberto Nepomuceno, (1864-1920). He differed from the earlier man Gomez, in that the latter's style and treatment was thoroughly Italian in character, and Nepomuceno has worked out his own technique.

Many composers have written operas on native stories and legends. The Argentinians have developed this idea so far that the government gives a yearly subsidy to the Buenos Aires opera house on condition that one new opera by a native composer shall be presented each season. Obviously these cannot always be of equal merit, but some of them have real distinction, and Felipe Boero's "El Matrero", a recent prize-winner, is outstanding. The subject is taken from *Gaucho* life, with a story not unlike that of "The Girl of the Golden West."

One of the latest prize-winners is called *Nazdah,* by a young Argentine named Athos Palma; another, called *Huemac,* is by Pascual de Rogatis. Vicente Forte is an extremely well trained musician, formerly a pupil of the Schola Cantorum in Paris and also of Felipe Pedrell in Spain. At this writing he is working on a music drama of which the setting is laid among the Incas at the time of the arrival of the Spaniards. This gives him the opportunity to inspire himself with both Indian and Mestizo material although he does not use actual themes. With his skillful treatment the pentatonic scale takes on as it were, new garments.

The Chilean musician, Humberto Allende, writes delightfully in the folk vein. He is fond of using dance rhythms without actually making transcriptions of tunes. In one orchestral composition he uses local street cries, and these simple fragments are thoroughly engaging when he has woven his spell over them. His work is well known and appreciated in Europe. Alfonso Leng and Prospero Bisquert are two among the other Chilean musicians who are making reputations for themselves beyond the confines of their own country.

Brazilian composers are working on nationalistic lines and though Fructosa Vianna is called by Brazilians the Ravel of Brazil, and Heitor Villa-Lobos is compared to Debussy, that does not mean that they are mere imitators, but that their points of view have resemblances. Paul Rosenfeld says of the music of Carlos Chavez that it has the directness and lack of oratorical flight of the Amerind, and that he is independent of programmes. Last, but far from least of the men whom we shall mention, is J. Octaviano Gonçalves, pianist, musicologist and composer of great talent. He has written in all the forms, using his knowledge of Brazilian folk-lore to good advantage.

In Nicaragua, Luis A. Delgadillo has composed among other things, an Incan Symphony which has reached international fame.

The compositions of the Cuban musician, Joseito White, are worthy of far wider diffusion than they have so far reached; and so on, but a list such as here set down makes no pretensions at being exhaustive. Other musicians are making experimental studies, as for instance, Julian Carillo in Mexico with his work on quarter tones. Everywhere there is vigor and freedom of viewpoint, and intellectual curiosity with spontaneity of approach.

In the light of this spirit of adventurous experimentation, the outlook is rich with promise, though the development is still new enough to make prognostication hazardous. The whole of Latin America has long been known and exploited by the older civilizations for its enormous material resources. Within the present generation Europe and North America are beginning to recognize the real importance of the Latin-American contributions to literature and the plastic and graphic arts. That the same recognition is not yet accorded to their music is due to other causes than to any inherent lack of worth in the music itself.

SONGS, DANCES, AND INSTRUMENTS OF SPANISH AMERICA

Songs or Dances found generally
(Spanish inheritance, but more or less altered)

Tirana   Folía, Zarabanda   Zapateado or Corrido or Ballad   Jota, Zapateo Alabanza   Fandango, Alborada

---

Argentine Uruguay, Paraguay

Songs
Vidala
Vidallta
Triste
Milonga
Estilo
Tonada

Dances
Cielo
Cielito
Tango
Zamba
Sombrerito
Tirana
Gato
Malambo
Caramba
Pericon
Chacarera
Media Caño del Campo

Chili

Songs
Tonada
Yaraví
Punto
Chilena
Catchua
Tirana

Songs
Cueca or Zamacueca
Gato
Pericon
Chacarera
Sombrerito
Caramba
Media caño del Campo
Cuando
Refalosa
Sajuriana

Brazil

Songs
Milonga
Modinha
Saudades
Caterete
Fado

Dances
Tango
Maxixe
Lundú
Bambula
Rumba
Batuque
Marote

Peru, Ecuador, Bolivia

Songs
Yaraví
Triste
Catchúa
Bambúco
Tonada
Marinera

Dances
Huanca
Huanea
Bundo
Pasillo
Guabina
Pampeña
Tendero
Reebalosa

Columbia, Venzuela, Central America

Songs
Joropo
Catchua
Bambuco
Merengue

Dances
Pasillo
Bunda
Habanera

Mexico

Songs
Mañanitas
Punto
Durazno
Palmero
Charapera
Son
Canovas

Dances
Jarabe Tapatio
Jarabe Gatuno
Catuno
Manola
Curripití
Ahuahulco
Caramba
Bamba
Tusa
Canelo
Habanera
Petenera
Guanábana
Danza
Telele
Contradanza

Carribean Islands

Songs
Son
Merengue
Rondé
Gulra
Balsté
Tambora
Contradanza
Guaracha

Dances
Danza
Rumba
Danzon
Bolero
Bamboula
Counjai
Calinda
Punto de Habana Cata or Chata
Guiouba

INSTRUMENTS found generally

flute, drum,   harp, castanets, (originally sea shells)   gourd rattles,   Guitar (3, 4, 5, or 6 strings, various local names)   trumpets

Local

(Argentine / Chili)
Trompe
Trutruca
Guimbarda or Birimbao
(A kind of Jews harp)
Cultrum
Pifilca (pipe)
Zampoña

(Peru, Ecuador, Bolivia) — *Local*
Quena
Charango (armadillo shell guitar)

(Columbia, Venzuela, Central America) — *Local*
Marimba
Maraca
Maruga (gourd)

(Mexico) — *Local*
Marimba
Mandolin
Bandolón
Salterio
Armadillo shell guitar

(Carribean Islands) — *Local*
Marimba
Tres

PARTIAL LIST OF MUSICIANS

It is impossible to make a list of musicians that could even approximate completeness, so the following list is offered with a definite recognition of its inadequacy.

Aguirre, J.	Argentine
Alas, C. de J.	Salvador
Allende, P. Humberto	Chile
Alomia Robles, D.	Peru
Anchorena, C. A.	Peru
Anckerman, J.	Cuba
Andrade, M. de	Brazil
Anitua, F.	Mexico
Astol, F.	Porto Rico
Bemberg, H.	Argentina
Benavente, J.	Bolivia
Berutti, A.	Argentina
Berutti, P.	Argentina
Bisquertt, P.	Chile
Boero, Felipe	Argentina
Braga, H.	Brazil
Broquá, A.	Uruguay
Bustamante, S.	Ecuador
Cabrera, A.	Argentina
Calvo, L. A.	Colombia
Campos, Ruben M.	Mexico
Carpio, R.	Peru
Carrasco, A.	Mexico
Carreño, Teresa	Venezuela
Carrillo, J.	Mexico
Casella, E. M.	Argentina
Castro, J. J.	Argentina
Castro, R.	Mexico
Caturla, A.	Cuba
Chavez, C.	Mexico
Conesa, Maria	Mexico
Cugat, Javier	Cuba
Curto, H.	Mexico
d'Alvarez, Margarita	Peru

Delgadillo, F...Nicaragua
Dente, D..Uruguay
Drangosch, F...Argentina
Duncker-Lavalle, Luis..Peru
Duran, Sixto...Ecuador
Eli, Justin...Haiti
Enriquez, J. P...Mexico
Esperon, I. F..Mexico
Espoile, R. H...Argentina
Fabini, F. E...Uruguay
Fonseca, J..Costa Rica
Forno, Alberto...Argentina
Forte, Vicente...Argentina
Fructosa, Vianna...Brazil
Gaito, Constantino...Argentina
Galimany, A...Panama
Gallet, Luciano..Argentina
Gil, J...Argentina
Gomez, C. G..Brazil
Grever, M...Mexico
Guerra, O..Brazil
Hahn, Reynaldo..Venezuela
Guerrero, A. G...Chile
Gutierrez, F...Porto Rico
Gutierrez, P. E...Venezuela
Jimenez, M..Cuba
Lecuona, E..Cuba
Leng, Alfonso...Chile
Lerdo de Tejada, M..Mexico
Lerena, E. H..Uruguay
Levy, Alexander..Brazil
Lopez Buchardo, C...Argentina
Machado, A..Argentina
Mojica, J...Mexico
Murillo, E..Colombia
Nepomuceno, Alberto...Brazil
Nieto, C. A..Costa Rica
Nieto, R...Mexico

Nin, Joaquín..Cuba
Novaes, Guiomar..Brazil
Nunes, Joao..Brazil
Octaviano, J...Brazil
Ortiz de Zarate, E..Chile
Oswald, E...Brazil
Palma, Athos..Argentina
Paniagua, R...Honduras
Pasques, V. A...Argentina
Pedrell, Carlos...Argentina
Pericás, J...Porto Rico
Pereyra, C...Chile
Ponce, Manuel M...Mexico
Posadas, G..Mexico
Quevedo, G...Colombia
Reyes, T. P...Mexico
Rocca, Angel..Argentina
Rogatis, Pascual de...Argentina
Roig, G..Cuba
Roldan, A..Cuba
Romero, J. C...Mexico
Romero, L. C..Cuba
Ruiz Espadero, N..Cuba
Sanchez de Fuentes, E...Cuba
San Malo..Panama
Santa Cruz Wilson, D..Chile
Schiuma, A. L..Argentina
Soro, Enrique...Chile
Tavárez, M. G...Porto Rico
Tello, R. J...Mexico
Traversari, P...Ecuador
Valderrama, C...Peru
Valle Riestra, J..Peru
Vega, A...Santo Domingo
Vega Matuo, A...Nicaragua
Velásquez, F. M...Mexico
Vigil y Robles, E...Mexico
Villa-Lobos, H..Brazil

Villalba Muñoz, P. A._____Peru
White, Joseito_____Cuba
Williams, Alberto_____Argentina
Zanelli, R._____Chile

BIBLIOGRAPHY

BIBLIOGRAPHY

ACOSTA, José de
   The Natural History of the Indians, 1604. Repub. 1880, Purchas Ed.

ALVARADO, P. de
   The Conquest of Guatemala. 1924 Ed.

ALVAREZ, J.
   Origenes de la música Argentina. 1908.

ANDERSON, C. L. G.
   Old Panama.

ANDRADE, M. de
   Ensayo sobre la música Brasileira. Sáo Paulo. 1923.

ANDREWS, Capt.
   Journey of Captain Andrews. 1827.

ARZENO, J.
   El folklore musical Dominicano.

AUSTIN, Mary
   The American Rhythm. 1923.

BANCROFT, H. H.
   Works.

BANDELIER, A. F.
   Notes on the Bibliography of Yucatan. 1881.
   The Indians and Aboriginal Ruins of Peru. 1907.

BÉCLARD-D'HARCOURT, M.
   Mélodies populaires Indiennes. 1923.
   La musique dans la Sierra Andine, Journal de la Soc. des Americanistes.
   La musique des Incas et ses survivances. 1925.

BENZONI, Girolamo
   Historia del Mundo nuevo, 1565.
   Americae, Pars Quarta, 1613. Also Hakluyt Ed. 1857.

BINGHAM, Hiram
   Inca Land. 1922.

BOURNE, E. G.
   Spain in America.

BRINTON, D. G.
   Works.

BRITO FREYRE, F. de
   Relacão de viagem. 1657. rep. 1925.

BROSSES, C. de
　　Histoire de Navigations. 1756.
BRYCE, James
　　South America, 1912.
CÁCERES, E. M.
　　Origen de la musica incaica. In Musica en America. 1921.
CÁCERES, V. G.
　　Cancionero incaico. 1929.
CALDERON DE LA BARCA, Mme. (given as Mme, *C* de la *B*.)
　　Life in Mexico. First Ed. 1843.
CAMPOS, R. M.
　　El folklore literario de Mexico. 1929.
　　El folklore y la musica mexicana. 1928.
CARPENTER, F. G.
　　Along the Parana.
CERNICHIARI, Vicenzo
　　Storia della musica nel Brazile. 1926.
CIEZA DE LEÓN
　　Chronicles of Peru. 2nd part. Ed of 1883.
　　Travels of Cieza de León part. Ed. of 1864.
　　Civil Wars in Peru. 1923.
CLAVIGERO, D. F. S.
　　The history of Mexico. Ed. of 1817.
CLEMENTS MARKHAM, R.
　　A History of Peru. 1892.
　　Rights and Laws of the Incas. Hakluyt Soc. 1873.
COESTER, Alfred
　　The Literary History of Spanish America. 1916.
COOPER, C. S.
　　Understanding South America. 1918.
CORTIJO ALAHIJA, L.
　　Musicologia Latino-Americana. La musica popular.
CUNNINGHAM-GRAHAM, R. B.
　　Life of Pedro de Valdivia
　　A Brazilian Mystic
DE BRY, Theodor
　　Admiranda Narratio, etc. 1590.

Latin America. 1634.

Brevis Narratio. 1591.

Americae, Pars Quarta.

DIAZ DE CASTILLO, Bernal
The Conquest of New Spain. Hakluyt Ed. 1908.

DOBRIZHOFFER, M.
An Account of the Abipones. 1822.

DOMINGUEZ, Francisco
Sones, Canciones y Corridos Michoacanas. 3 quarto pamphlets.

DUDLEY, R.
Dell' Arcano del Mare. 1646-7.

ENGELHART, C. A.
The Missions and Missionaries of California. 1908-15.

ESPINOSA, A. M.
Works.

EWBANK,T.
Life in Brazil. 1856.

FERNANDEZ DE OVIEDO Y VALDÉS
Cronica de las Indias. 1547.

FLETCHER and KIDDER
Brazil and the Brazilians. 1866.

FORD, J. B. M.
Brazilian Literature. 1922.

FORTE, Vicente
El canto popular. 1923.

FRÉZIER, A. F.
A Voyage to the South Sea. 1717.

FRITZ, Samuel
Journal of Travel of Father Fritz. Hakluyt Ed. 1922.

FRIEDENTHAL, A.
Stimmen der Völker. 1911.

FURT, J.
Coreografia Gauchesa. 1927.

GAGE, Thomas
A New Survey of the West Indies. 1648.

GANN, Thomas
Ancient Cities and Modern Tribes.

GARCÍA CUBAS, A.
El libro de mis recuerdos.

GARCÍA, DE MOGUER
Los viages de Diego García. Ed. of 1908.

GARCÍA DE PALACIO
Carta al Rey de España. 1860.

GARCíA ICAZBALCETA, J.
Bibliografia Mexicana. 1886.

GARCILASO DE LA VEGA
Royal Commentaries of Peru. Ricaut Translation, 1688.

GENET, J.
Esquisse d'une civilization oubilée. 1927.

GRUBB, K. C.
Amazon and Andes.

GUMILLA, Padre, J.
El Orinoco ilustrado. 1745

HALL, Capt. Basil
Extracts from a Journal written on the Coasts of Chile, Peru
and Mexico. 1824.

HARRISSE, H.
Bibliotheca Americana Vetustissima. 1866.

HELPS, Arthur
The Spanish Conquest in America. 1900.

HRDLIČKA, A.
Early Man in South America. 1912.

HUDSON, W. H.
Far Away and Long Ago. 1918.

HULSIUS, L.
Die fünfte kurze wunderbahre Beschreibung. 1683.

HUMBOLDT, A. von
Political Essay of the Kingdom of New Spain. 1811.
Personal Narrative. 1815.

JAGOR, F.
Reisen in den Philippinen. 1873.

JAMES, E. O.
Primitive Ritual and Belief.

JOUTEL, H.
Journal Historique.
A Journal of the Last Voyage, etc., etc. 1713.

JOYCE, T. A.
South American Archaeology. 1912.
KELLER, F.
The Amazon and Madura Rivers.
KING EDWARD, LORD KINGSBOROUGH
Antiquities of Mexico. 1831-48.
KROEBER, A. L.
Peoples of the Philippines. 1928.
LANDA, Bishop F. M. S.
Historia de Yucatan durante la dominación Española.
LANGE, A.
In the Amazon Jungle. 1912.
LA PEROUSE
Voyage de la Perouse autour du monde. 1797.
LA CASAS, B.
Brevissima Relacion, etc. 1552. repr.
LOPEZ COGOLLUDO, D.
Historia de Yucatan. 1688.
LOPEZ, DE GOMARA, F.
La historia general de las Indias. 1554.
Historia de Mexico. 1554.
LUCE, Allena
Canciones Populares. (Puerto Rico). 1921.
LUMHOLTZ, C.
Unknown Mexico. 1902.
LUMMIS, C. F.
The Land of Poco Tiempo.
LYNCH, Ventura R.
Cancionero Bonaerense. 1925.
MAGALHÕES DE GANDAVO
The History of Brazil. Ed. of 1922.
MASON, Gregory
Green Gold of Yucatan.
MAUDSLAY, A.
A Glimpse of Guatemala.
MAWE, J.
Travels in the Interior of Brazil. 1816.
MENDIZABAL, M. O. de
Ensayos sobre las civilizaciones aborigenes Americanas.

MENENDEZ PIDAL, R.
　Las España del Cid.
MEAD, C. M.
　Old Civilizations of Inca Land. 1924.
MEANS, P. A.
　Ancient Civilizations of the Andes. 1931.
MELLO, G. T. P. de
　A musica no Brasil. 1908.
MORLEY, S. G.
　The Historical Value of the Books of Chilam Balam.
NASH, Roy
　The Conquest of Brazil. 1922.
NAVARRETE, M. F.
　Examen historico de los viajes. 1849.
NUTTALL, Zelia
　Codex Nuttall. 1902.
PAGÉS, B. M. F.
　Travels round the World. 1791.
PAN AMERICAN UNION SERIES
　Seeing South America.
　Bulletins.
PASQUES, V. A.
　Texto de musica.
PEDRELL, F.
　Diccionario biografico.
PEÑAFIEL, A.
　Cantares Mexicanos.
　Coleccion de documentos
PIGAFETTA, F. A.
　Magellan's Voyage around the World. Ed. of 1906.
PONS, F. R. J. de.
　A Voyage to the Eastern Part of South America. 1806.
POUND, Louise
　The Beginnings of Poetry
PRESCOTT, W. H.
　The Conquest of Peru.
　The Conquest of Mexico.

REDFIELD, Robert
Tepoztlan, a Mexican Village. 1930.
RIBERA, J.
La Musica de las Cantigas. 1922.
ROBLES, D. Alomia
Works
ROJAS, Ricardo
Le literatura Argentina 1917.
El canto popular. 1923.
ROOSEVELT, Theodore
Through the Brazilian Wilderness.
RUEDA, J. G.
Musica y bailes criollos de la Argentina. From Musica en America. 1921.
SAAVEDRA GUZMAN, A. de
El Peregrino Indiano. 1599. repr. 1880.
SAHAGUN, B.
Historia general de las cosas de Nueva España.
SARMIENTO DE GAMBOA, P.
Viaje al estrecho de Magellanes. 1768.
The Diary of Ulric Schmidel. Purchas his Pilgrimes.
SEDGWICK, H. D.
A Short History of Spain. 1929.
SOLIS, A. de
History of Mexico. 1691.
SPELL, Lota
Music and Instruments of the Aztecs. Reprint from M. T. N. A. 1925.
SQUIER, E. G.
Nicaragua, its People, Scenery and Monuments. 1860.
Notes on Central America. 1855.
STEPHENS, J. L.
Incidents of Travel in Yucatan. 1848.
Incidents of Travel in Central America. 1848.
TALAMON, G. O.
Un cuarto de siglo de musica Argentina.
TORRE, J. M. de la
La Habana antigua y moderna.

TREND, J. B.
  The Music of Spanish History. 1926.
  All books written by Trend about Spain.
VEGA, Carlos
  La Musica de un codice colonial. 1931.
VENEGAS, M.
  Juan Maria de Salvatierra. Ed. of 1929.
  El Apostol Mariano. 1754.
von TSCHUDI, J. J.
  Travels in Peru. Ross translation. 1849.
WAFER, Lionel
  A New Voyage and Description of the Isthmus of America. 1699.
WALLS y MERINO, M.
  La Musica popular de las Filipinas.
WILLARD, T. A.
  The City of the Sacred Well. 1926.
WISSLER, Clark
  The American Indian. 1922.
  Various Guide Books, periodicals, etc., from most of the countries included in the book.

COLOPHON

This book is printed on Strathmore Cockatoo lightweight paper from 11-point Granjon set on the Linotype machine. Cincinnati initials and handset Civilite chapter headings. Frontispiece hand cut rubber blocks. Presswork by Mr. Jack H. Reed. Composition by Mr. Willard E. Francis. Layout, design, and typography by Mr. Thomas E. Williams, Santa Ana Fine Arts Press.